What Makes a Man a Hero?

STORIES ABOUT MEN FOR FATHER'S DAY

Daphne Simpkins

Copyright © 2020 Daphne Simpkins.

All rights reserved. No part of this publication may be reproduced, distributed or transmitted in any form or by any means, including photocopying, recording, or other electronic or mechanical methods, without the prior written permission of the publisher, except in the case of brief quotations embodied in critical reviews and certain other noncommercial uses permitted by copyright law. For permission requests, write to the publisher, addressed "Attention: Permissions Coordinator," at the address below.

Daphne Simpkins/Quotidian Books

What Makes a Man a Hero?/ Daphne Simpkins

ISBN 978-1-7320158-4-5

Contents

What Makes a Man a Hero? 5

1 Most Unforgettable Character 11

2 Mr. Ashley 19

3 The Beauty Room 43

4 Legacy of a Very Handy Man 51

5 Barking Dogs & Dead Peacocks 57

6 Joy Ride with the Boys 65

7 Secret Agent Man 71

8 Two Shakes of a Lamb's Tail 75

9 Baby Toss 83

10 Safe at Home 87

11 Observe the Man 91

12 Hello, My Brother 95

13 When God Smiles 99

14 My Cranky Valentine 105

15 Fever Pitch 109

16 Missing Piece of Nora's Cake ... 113

17 Her Bodyguard 123

18 What He Wants for Father's Day 129

19 Before there was Mr. Lovejoy... there was this man 135

20 Bonus Excerpt: Lovejoy 137

21 Books by Daphne Simpkins 171

About Daphne Simpkins 173

For Jody and Julie Helms

What Makes a Man a Hero?

When my claustrophobic sister Julie Ann and her down-in-the-back husband Jody were trapped on a stalled elevator in a posh hotel, they were not alone in their distress. Two young male execs were with them. As soon as the elevator lurched heart-stoppingly close to a place near a floor level, the two young men were able to wedge open the elevator door just enough to squeeze up and through. The two executives escaped, leaving behind my sister-- a grandmother-- and her husband Jody, her hero.

I heard from my sister that, "Jody couldn't believe his eyes--two young men leaving me behind! But my Jody, with his back hurting, pushed me up and out through the tight elevator doors and then he pulled himself up and out. I was crying by then. You know how I can't bear closed-in places. Once we were out of there, my Jody put me in a chair and said, 'Sit tight. I'm gonna get you a biscuit and a cup of coffee.'"

He did--her hero with the bad back.

Our hero, too.

For that single story of Jody's faithful care and resilience is not the only story of his heroism that pervades family life. Like most heroic men, he endures, and the stories of his endurance are like other family's fathers and men who take care of their families and of family business.

Family lore captures the stories of all kinds of men and fathers who are inherently, because of their very nature and integrity, daily heroes. Most families have a story they treasure but keep to themselves about the man in the family who is a hero and what he did that gained him that label.

Often, he has not pulled someone from a stalled elevator or saved children from a burning orphanage. His actions are frequently, routinely much more ordinary, heroic feats camouflaged in the dailyness of making a good life with the people he loves more than himself. Being this kind of hero doesn't have much to do with bringing anyone flowers (though a posy is always welcome) or candy (Hershey's kisses) or taking out the trash without being asked. The truly heroic men simply put the safety and comfort of others before their own safety and comfort, are alert to ways to protect and care for the people around them, and will do whatever is necessary however they are personally feeling to fulfill their self-appointed mission of protecting the homeplace and the people who trust him to do just that.

They are extraordinary, ordinary men. While they are unforgettable, their stories don't get told very often. But I'll tell you a powerful secret. When a woman experiences the tender mercies of a man like that, she never quite gets over it.

As I approach Father's Day this year, I think of all these men--and my own father-- and especially of Jody who rescued my sister from the trapped elevator car and of what she said afterwards: "My Jody couldn't believe it—how those two younger men could leave the elevator with a lady still trapped on board. Those two young men in their business suits never looked back. After my Jody got us out of there, he never left my side."

Jody is her husband, but my sister knew what kind of man he is because she was raised by another extraordinary, ordinary man: our dad.

And we have known others. What follows are some of their stories. And you may have seen some of them before in different collections of essays or in newspapers and magazines.

Many of those newspapers and Sunday magazine sections have vanished. Others have morphed becoming different technologically driven publishing vehicles for storytelling.

Some of the essays collected here were written then about my father, and a handful of them appeared in the first memoir I wrote about family life in the South: *The Long Good Night.* That book has recently been released in paperback and is still available as an e-book and on Kindle. But a couple of those essays belonged in a book that celebrates men as heroes. I extend my gratitude to W. B. Eerdmans Publishing Co. for allowing me to include them here. Those essays are: "My Most Unforgettable Character" and "Legacy of a Very Handy Man."

Since that first memoir I have written other books that included essays about my father and the men I have known, admired and loved. From *A Cookbook for Katie*, I've excerpted: "My Cranky Valentine," "Fever Pitch," "Safe at Home," "Baby Toss," and "In Two Shakes of a Lamb's Tail."

From the recent book *BLESSED*, which is about caregiving, I have excerpted an essay about the first man I ever loved outside of my family, "Mr. Ashley."

So, you may have encountered some of these essays before, but this year I wanted to take the time to assemble these pieces that appeared in a variety of other sources into one volume to celebrate Father's Day the way a grateful daughter, friend, and sister-in-law does who knows the difference between an extraordinary, ordinary heroic man and that other guy.

1
Most Unforgettable Character

"Bon Jour. Bon soir. C'est moi." I flung a few French phrases over my shoulder as I gathered my books to head to my French class. I had a hard time pronouncing foreign words and attempted to ameliorate my insecurity by saying the words to anyone near me before I actually had to do it in front of Madame Hill and my classmates.

"Bon jour to you too," Daddy replied, rising from his desk, where he had been reading, to walk me to the door. He often did that—escorted me to the door when I was leaving, and then from the doorway he would call a few familiar sayings of his own after me: *Be careful. It's easy to have an accident. One moment of thoughtlessness is enough to ruin the rest of your life.*

Today my sweet daddy didn't warn me about anything. He asked a question instead. "The *Reader's Digest* says that all children have a particular memory of a parent that is theirs alone. Do you have a special memory of me?"

The mantel clock snuffled rather than chimed because Daddy had muffled the bell. We had not liked the clock's noisy reminder that time was passing. This whimpering event was still loud enough to remind me that I had to get to my class.

"I can't think of anything," I replied quickly.

"The *Reader's Digest* says you can," he asserted, moving further out the door. It wasn't that he didn't believe me. It was that he didn't believe that the *Reader's Digest* could ever be wrong.

I shrugged the way a young college woman studying French does when she wants to appear to be living a more adventurous life than she really is.

Daddy stood in the doorway, watching me back out of the driveway, and I could feel his mind racing ahead to the challenges of my day. I waved good-bye to him over the steering wheel as the warnings recycled in both of our minds simultaneously: *Be careful at the intersection next to Richardson's Pharmacy. People often try to scoot through that light. Lock your car doors once you're inside. Pay attention to what's going on around you. Check your gas gauge. There is no excuse for running out of gas because if you need gas money, all you have to do is ask me for it.*

I chose the long way to French class, through the old neighborhood where F. Scott Fitzgerald had courted Zelda. I liked the slow way to most places—a key to my nature that I hid from others the same way I pretended to my family that I was smarter in college than I really was. I was thinking with dread about the day's French test when suddenly the steering wheel trembled in my hand. A thumping began. I eased up on the gas. Daddy had been warning me for years that this could happen. I had a flat tire.

"Mon Dieu!" I exclaimed, slowing to the curb.

I opened the trunk, spied the jack and the spare, and I remembered everything Daddy had taught me: I was supposed to pry off the hubcap, jack up the car, twist loose the lug nuts, lift off the flat tire, and put on the doughnut spare. But all I could do was say out loud, "I can't do that."

Instead, I walked to a nearby house, asked to use the phone of one of those strangers who might kill me, went right on inside the house where danger lurked to the phone and called my Daddy. I told him where I was and what had happened.

I felt his adrenaline rush in response to my call for help. His voice got stronger, and he said, "Get out of that stranger's house right now. Go back to the car and wait for me. I'll be right there."

I thanked the stranger for the use of the phone and went back to the car to wait for Daddy. He didn't appear right away, and I grew warm in the morning sun. I was already late to class, and my anxiety about the test intensified when I realized that I would have to take a make-up. Surely that would be harder.

Nervous, I was scanning the far end of the street for Daddy's Cadillac when I saw Daddy jog around the corner and run toward me in his good blue-and-burgundy business suit.

When he saw me, Daddy waved exuberantly. Then, after he knew I was safe, his body relaxed, and he gave himself over to the physicality of running, enjoying his own strength and motion.

I resisted the impulse to run toward him. It was always my impulse, but I was a college girl studying French, after all.

Daddy saw me hold back, but he kept running toward me anyway, smiling broadly. When he reached me, he was laughing at himself and with relief that I was all right. "When you called, I got in such a hurry that I locked myself out of the house and my car. I'll need a lift home."

"I couldn't change the tire," I explained. "I know you taught me how, but I don't have the strength in my arms." It was a limp lie. I hadn't even tried.

He waved aside my apology. "As long as one of us can do it, we're all right." It was what he always said when he helped me.

Positioning the crowbar I had retrieved from the trunk, Daddy said, "If you can't reach me the next time you have a flat tire, use your foot this way to create leverage with the crowbar. Your leg is stronger than your arm. Kick it like this. Of course, girls don't often wear the right kind of shoes for this maneuver." He took his dressy handkerchief out of his suit pocket and wiped his hands on it as if it were an old rag.

I smiled apologetically, a girl wearing the wrong kind of shoes.

"You're all dressed up," I acknowledged ruefully. "Am I making you late for an appointment?"

"You could never make me late for anything that matters to me more than you do," he replied.

We worked in silence then. I handed him the tools as he asked for them. It was a familiar pattern. Ever since I had been a little girl, I had been his number-one helper.

He finished the job, putting the flat tire in the trunk and securing the jack so that it wouldn't rattle. "I'll get the flat tire fixed for you," he offered.

"I could take it somewhere," I proposed weakly.

"You can when you don't have me to do it for you," he said.

I nodded my thanks as he got in the passenger seat. It was a short drive home. I parked in our driveway, and Daddy opened the car door and looked at me sheepishly. "I need you to unlock the side door to my office."

I followed him on that well-worn path from the car to the side door. Each footstep forward was also a step backward in time. Each step brought a memory. The first kiss from my boyfriend—and the last. The night Mary Ellen came knocking on my window when her son Matthew was about to be born. The countless times I heard Daddy's footsteps crunch the gravel on his way to work the midnight shift at the air force base.

"There are my keys!" Daddy announced when I opened the door. He was relieved that his key ring had not disappeared. Things did that around him sometimes. But there they were, right on top of the *Reader's Digest*, which lay open to the essay he had been reading earlier.

Daddy's still-unanswered question about a signature memory of him rose up between us. Embarrassed that he had asked, Daddy fumbled with the magazine and placed it on the stack of reading materials that he kept to take to hospitals and to people confined at home. It was near the wall map of the state of Alabama and his big green filing cabinet, where he stored all his memorabilia.

I wanted to tell him that I remembered working with him at the old apartment building on Alabama Street that he had renovated and how we collected the rent together. That I remembered how, when he left to work the midnight shift at the air force base, he came by my bedroom window and tapped on the glass with his fingertips to tell me good night because he could see I was still reading. My light was on.

"Is there something else?" Daddy asked as he felt me linger in the shadows of his office. The mantel clock made its muffled sound, and we both looked at it, surprised that it kept trying to proclaim the passing of time with its bell swaddled in cotton.

I pointed toward the *Reader's Digest.* "I'll always remember how you ran toward me in your good suit today—in a hurry to reach me. And you always say, 'As long as one of us can do it, we're all right.' I'll remember that," I promised him.

He smiled diffidently, glad and a little embarrassed to think that I had gained my special memory of him only that day. But I hadn't.

He was right before. The *Reader's Digest* was right too.

I remembered my daddy.

I remembered everything.

2
Mr. Ashley

Dad was twenty-one years old when he converted an old Southern mansion into an apartment building and himself into a landlord. The building he called by its street address Alabama Street stretched through the city block and was within walking distance of downtown Montgomery, Al. Renting out apartments was a way of supporting himself and his mama, Florine Acosta--a woman we girls—his four daughters-- were taught to call Flo.

Alabama Street was seductive in a quintessential Southern way, with varying levels of many different shapes of rooms. There were four entrances, one on each side of the building. Two of these entrances led into the heart of the building--a hallway broad enough to be called a lobby.

Three interior apartments branched off of this hallway and to the wide brown stairs which led upstairs to three more apartments. There were two exterior apartments: Number One faced the parallel Scott Street. Apartment Number Nine was off to itself on the side of the building. The downstairs apartments had private entrances, and tenants paid more for these. More than one natural law was born on Alabama Street, but the first one that I recall is: *Privacy always costs more.*

A variety of people lived there. Virginia lived there with her young son, Andy. When she abandoned him, my parents took him in to live with us for a year until she returned and took him back. For a whole year, we had a brother.

A woman upstairs committed suicide. She used a gun. I heard the shot in the middle of the night, and later in my life when I saw Tennessee Williams' play, "A Streetcar Named Desire," I sympathized with Blanche DuBois, who retained the memory of a gunshot in her mind. That blast of pain and release occurred over and over, taxing Blanche's mental strength. I carried forward in my own life the memory of that resonating gun shot that afflicted the fictional immortal Blanche and the echo of that other gun shot a tenant of Alabama Street created and which I heard as a child. Make-believe people and real people merged in my mind as equally authentic human touchstones of truth.

Two women who were waitresses at the Seven Seas restaurant downtown also lived on Alabama Street, and they were the wrong kind of women who wore the wrong kind of underwear. We knew because they didn't hang their dainties over the shower rod in the privacy of their bathrooms, which would have been the smart thing to do.

They hung their intimate undergarments on the communal clothesline outside where everyone saw them, which was "Dumb, dumb, dumb," my mother said. They were the kind of party girls who liked beer more than nice women were supposed to. They liked beer as much as my Daddy's mother Flo liked beer, which was too much.

The residents came and went on Alabama Street, complimenting the cleanliness of it and the choice of furniture when they first moved in. The closer it got to the end of the month, the more complaints they had. By the time they left owing two or more months' rent, the apartment always needed repainting, the mattresses needed to be replaced, and cigarette burns speckled most of the table tops.

"It's a miracle someone hasn't burned us down," my father repeatedly commented. And when he replaced the light bulbs, which were often taken by people who left like thieves in the night, he added sorrowfully, mourning for the nature of the people who had robbed him rather than his own loss over what was stolen: "Your mama and I would furnish these units better if people weren't such natural-born thieves. But the nicer the quality of furnishings, the more damage people do to them. What they don't destroy, they steal. We need to get the military people to live here. They respect property."

There were two air force bases in Montgomery, and my father was acutely attracted to the order and standards of behavior instituted in the military. He respected the personnel who were either stationed in town or were brought in temporarily to attend the officers' school over at Maxwell Air Force Base. "They have housing lists posted on those bases, and if we can ever get on those lists, we'll attract some good-paying tenants who won't steal from us or burn us down."

More than once, my father cast a thankful glance in the direction of the fire station across the street where the men who waited for the next emergency played dominoes with each other and sometimes a game of catch in the street with me. I was not allowed to bother the firemen, but if asked, I could play ball.

Generally, I was not allowed to talk with other adults. When a person older than I initiated a conversation, I was expected to answer in short responses, like "No, sir," and "Thank you." That was all.

If I did more than that, my behavior attracted the attention of my mother who usually began one of her lessons in decorum this way, "You know I don't have dumb children."

A natural law emerged from my mother's preliminary commentary to chastisement: *Having good manners proved we were not dumb.* But we weren't expected to talk much either.

It also meant that we had the brand of pride that separated us from the kind of people we did not want to be: *poor white trash.* The South was a stratified society, and poor white trash represented the lowest rung on the ladder. Poor people fit in the next higher category. Then, there was the working class. Middle class people followed. It was the group everyone wanted to belong to for it was accessible and the word *middle* was almost a synonym for American. Later in my life, I heard and read a great deal about discrimination against blacks and Jews in the South, but as a child growing up in Montgomery during the Civil Rights movement, my knowledge of segregated groups was tied to wealth, work, education, and good manners rather than color of skin or religion.

My family just barely inched our way out of the working class and into the middle class, and though many people falsely assumed that we had plenty of money because Daddy owned an apartment building, we had to work very hard at keeping ourselves eligible to belong to this group of middle-class people. Membership was not formal; you belonged if other people thought of you as middle class.

Without money or a good social background to help lever us up the social ladder, we did what many middle class people do in order to gain and keep a preferred place in a society: we specialized in having and exercising common sense, and we showed it through our good manners and by making good grades in school. Then perversely, in a move that is as common as a Southern rebel's bent toward self-destruction through gallant acts, we ostracized ourselves from the wealthier people whose company we unconsciously courted by displaying too great a tolerance for eccentric behaviors in others.

My father said that as Christians we were commanded not to judge people, but the expansiveness we felt for the tenants of Alabama Street and the members of our own complex clan of crazy-acting kinfolk was larger than the rules of decorum allowed, and in the South those boundaries are generous. My family did live more than just a double life, moving in and out of the social worlds that varied in ranges of presentability. We kept company with ex-cons and righteous people; we lived among the sober and the drunk, and we had fellowship with the very poor and the dark of skin and the well-to-do and the whitest folks. We were as comfortable in one group as another. If we had been truly refined, we would have felt a sense of distance from the strangers on Alabama Street, but we did not, and people who were better bred and higher up on the social ladder saw that in us and kept their distance from us

While we lived on Alabama Street, I was immensely happy. I liked the building my father had transformed into a home for so many people who worked hard like he did. I was proud of him and what I considered his invention of that huge home place for so many people who needed a home. It was very big. I was as impressed with the size of it as I was the elements of architectural beauty that were aspects of the building's personality, its seductive allure. There were fascinating turns and banisters to slide down and French doors and transoms and stained-glass windows.

Best of all, there was a small room underneath the ground floor stairwell where a child-sized door led to what became my secret room. I worked there with my drawing tools in the small room where I also stored my broom and dust pan after I had swept the hallway and the front porch, a job that had to be done every day.

I liked sweeping as I liked most kinds of labor. I particularly loved cleaning the stairs. I was only allowed to go upstairs to sweep, and entering the forbidden terrain of the next floor up lent the work a kind of mystery and excitement of being in the foreign world of strangers on the floor where I was not otherwise allowed. I took my time walking up the stairs each day, savoring the ascent, pausing to listen-- to hear what was going on behind closed doors. I was a natural born eavesdropper, and I have never felt guilty about listening in on other people's lives. It was a trait I evidenced as a child, and which I never gave up.

I knew the people who lived on Alabama Street by sight, although not all of them knew who I was or really ever saw me. As a child, I was invisible to many people and patted on the head or offered a stick of gum by others who sensed my presence as one does a light breeze blowing by.

Mr. Ashley was different. He knew me. He saw me. He lived in Apartment Number 3 on what was called the ground floor, but it was really one flight up from street level. The stairs were wide and not steep, but they were still a challenge for him. He walked stiffly in what appeared to be his entire wardrobe: tweedy gray suits with dress shirts. The collars of his shirts were frayed and a faded white. They uncannily matched his thin course yellow-white hair.

In the beginning of our friendship, Mr. Ashley did not leave Alabama Street very often, and so he was starved for any news I could bring him. Sometimes, when I finished sweeping the hallway, he brought me a Nehi grape drink, and I told him which of his neighbors had company the night before for dinner, and who was moving in and who was moving out.

Occasionally, Mr. Ashley asked me to do a small chore for him, like change a light bulb or reach something that had fallen and rolled underneath his couch. He could not stoop or stretch easily. He spent most of his time sitting in a chair by his window, for his apartment looked out over Scott Street, which ran behind Alabama Street.

From his kitchen, Mr. Ashley could watch the fire station and the fire trucks come and go and his neighbors dart into the Scott Street grocery. He watched when they took their trash to the garbage cans that fitted snugly into the back-left corner of the side yard.

Sometimes, I took Mr. Ashley's trash out for him because it was a long walk from his apartment to the trash cans; and those times, he usually offered me another cold drink—sometimes orange, sometimes strawberry. Although I knew both my parents would not approve, I accepted.

I took slow sips of the fruit drink because Mr. Ashley gave them to me to buy himself some time with some company, and I, a working man's child, wanted him to get his money's worth. During one of our conversations, he told me his deepest secret. "My dream these days is to take a walk outside again."

I said immediately that I could go only as far as the street corner alone without my mother's permission, and he said, "My dear, I don't think I can travel so far," and I promised, "We could go slow."

He smiled fearfully, and his lips were dry and his teeth were his own--they didn't click when he talked--and they were yellowed, like his hair.

We didn't take a walk that day.

And we didn't walk the next day. I had to tell Mr. Ashley that I had raked the front yard, and he had to say that he would come and see what I had done, and then I had to say that they were working on the street two blocks down, but I couldn't tell what they were doing, and he said maybe he could figure it out, and then I had to say, "Would you, 'cause I'm curious?" and he nodded cautiously, determinedly, as if he were ready to do me a favor for a change.

It took us a long time to reach the front door of the lobby, and in order to make it look like I walked slow all the time, I explained to Mr. Ashley how the light passing through the stained glass window in the foyer could turn my skin different shades of colors, and he smiled faintly. While he was standing in the sunlight, he closed his eyes as if he were bathing in the colors, and I closed my eyes too, and he said, "I can hear them," and I said, "I hear them too," because sometimes when I stood in the colored light I could hear angels singing, but no one had ever mentioned it to me, so I didn't bring it up.

Mr. Ashley was the only person in my life who ever admitted he could hear angels singing, and I never forgot it. When the angels caught their breath, Mr. Ashley and I each caught ours, and we moved in sequence out the front door and across the wide gray porch and then down the flight of stairs that led to the street.

He did not lean on me. He gripped his cane, the fingers of his hand pale and not callused or rough like my father's who did what he called *the real work of the world.* Then, I whispered a prayer to God that Mr. Ashley and I could think of ourselves as walking on water, an idea that I got out of the Bible. The notion that the ground could be turned into water rose up in me like a giggle that wants to come out, but I kept my mouth closed shut, forgetting that I had told Mr. Ashley that some men were working two blocks away, and I didn't know what they were doing. I was surprised when he answered the original question.

"They are lifting out the cobblestones to get to the water line, I think," Mr. Ashley explained suddenly. "Those old red cobblestones came to town as ballast on ships from the old country. You won't see them on just any street, and they will last a whole lot longer than asphalt."

"You know a lot about streets?" I asked, as we turned and casually began the slow walk back to the house as if we hadn't done anything special. I remembered that later: what a miracle feels like —ordinary and extraordinary at the same time. It didn't have to be like the parting of the Red Sea; it could feel like a slow walk with an old man in the sunshine.

"I used to know a little something about everything," he replied, sucking in his cheeks.

I think something inside of him must have started to hurt, because we didn't talk after that, except I think we were both praying silently. The angels started humming.

Once we were back at the base of the front steps, he closed his eyes, and his head went back an inch, and I wasn't worried for even a second that he was about to faint. I know what it's like to want to feel the sun on your face and give in to that craving. Sometimes, I just stand still in the sunshine, and when I do, I think: *I feel love.* And I don't know exactly what I mean by that, except sometimes words come out of me that I don't plan to think or say, but I trust what the Bible calls *utterances*.

After our first walk, Mr. Ashley was too tired to give me a cold drink from his ice box, and I was disappointed because I felt like I had earned a reward. It was only years later when I realized that desiring a reward for showing that you love others is not exactly a sin, but it is a fatal error in expectation, because a lot of the time loving others doesn't give anything back, including something simple like a grape drink.

I left Mr. Ashley alone, without saying his name again, and I closed the door quietly behind me. I knew that he would take a nap, but it was going to be a dreaming sleep that would build his strength. As I walked away, I whispered to God, "Please don't let him be afraid anymore."

My parents were unaware of the extent of my friendship with Mr. Ashley, although at night when they heard my prayers, I included his name at the end of the long list of relatives. When my daddy went to collect the rent, he sometimes took me with him because he said he wanted me *to see how the other side lived.* It took me a while to learn that the other side he was referring to were the people who did not pay their bills on time.

Invisible standing next to Daddy, I could hear the number of excuses people made to explain why they weren't able to pay their rent on time. They didn't speak to me. From their view, I did not exist. They were too concentrated on explaining why they were short on cash or needed five more days to pay.

My father was patient and understanding, but he had an opinion about how people could avoid living on the other side. "Honey, when you grow up, and you're living on your own--with a husband or without and I'll be the first to tell you, you don't ever have to get married--the first bill you pay is your tithe. That decision alone will solve most of your financial problems. Good stewardship of God's blessings is your number one job. Pay your bills in the order of their priority. Next, make your house payment. Then, put a little something in savings. Everything else follows. Utilities. Then, food. Then, clothing. If you have some money left, give yourself a little bit of pocket money. You don't need much. Having pocket money so that you don't feel desperate for it can save you a lot of spending mistakes. That's hard to understand, but you can take my word for it. If you feel like you've got some money in your pocket, you won't do foolish things pretending you have more than you do."

Mr. Ashley was one of the tenants who always paid his rent promptly. When we stopped at his door, he opened it immediately, handing my father a small beige envelope with his name imprinted on the back flap and the exact rent amount in cash (fifty-five dollars), and he never nodded to me particularly though we were keenly aware of one another. Only as we walked away, I peeked back over my shoulder, and his eyes filled with gladness and joy and his attention followed all the steps that I took, and I knew that Mr. Ashley loved me.

Mr. Ashley was the first person I ever loved outside of my family. Though I have no proof of it, I loved him, and I know he loved me.

During the monthly rent collection, my father routinely inspected the hallway for debris and burned out light bulbs. I looked forward to going on the inspection tour with my father. I liked to be the one beside him, for he walked with confidence and energy, and he often laughed at what I said, and I loved to be the one who made him laugh. He could grow serious though, and once he became very solemn right before he complimented my work. My father preached a prophecy over me that day. He said that I would always be a happy person. "You're smart enough to know that you are fighting a losing battle cleaning up after people, but you don't ever worry about it and you don't complain. Every day, you just go and sweep it all up again. I notice that about you. That's very wise," he approved.

I didn't worry about the messes made every day. I moved the day's collection of dirt and trash from one step to the next, enjoying the solitude, the sense of accomplishment, and the colored lights passing through the stained-glass window which marked the division in floors midway between the two levels. Some days, I took my rest at that midpoint where the light spilled color at my feet, and I listened for the angels.

Whether I could hear them or not, I knew the angels were there just as the tenants lived behind their closed doors in the many rooms that were all around me. My father never heard them. I know because some days on our tour he began to hum, and it was never what the angels were humming; then, he would start to sing, and it was never what the angels were singing, and they always stopped in their singing out of respect for his song. The angels of heaven always stood still in silence when my father began to sing. Lustrous voice! Shimmering sounds!

Praises to heaven for beauty! Praises to heaven.... the internal voice that wanted to cheer the presence of beauty chanted in response when my father sang. The angels and I listened to him sing: "Ah, sweet mystery of life at last I've found you. Ah, at last I know the secret of it all...."

Daddy might have known the secret of it all, but he didn't know the angels were singing, or he wouldn't have verbally trampled all over them. My father was not a rude man, but he was, it seemed to me, deaf to the sounds of heaven sometimes although he preached the hope of it. He was not a regular preacher. He only preached full-time for five years without pay to help a church get planted, but once they were set, we went back to our regular church, where he was the stand-in preacher, a position he assumed with great humility because he had never gone to college and had not even finished high school. His ability to speak well was based partly on his expressive golden voice, but his messages were inspired by the books that he read over and beyond the Bible, which he said he drank from every day. His respect for learning was great. He read continuously, living out one more of his early lessons intended for me: *You can learn anything you want to know if you can read.*

Most of my father's reading efforts were spent filling in the gaps of his education so he could earn a living that supported his large family. He finally got a job working the midnight shift at Maxwell Air Force Base. He was in charge of what they called the physical plant. He had a fancy title, but his mission was simple: If something broke, he fixed it. He never had a formal class or a day's training in any of the skills that he used: electrical, plumbing, carpentry. He had a problem-solving mind, and he could use it to solve any problem.

Because he was very good at repairing and fixing things, neighbors often called on him for help. He stayed busy all the time. He never accepted any pay for helping neighbors, friends, or even the needy friends of his friends. I rarely saw him rest. Sometimes, I wondered if my father ever stopped in his work to feel the sun on his face like Mr. Ashley and I did, or did he ever marvel at the symmetry and textures created by beveled glass and symmetrical configurations that framed the mosaics of rich colors that belonged in a church but which were part of Alabama Street?

Did my father ever caress the ruby red and royal blue hues of the glass, oh, and the golden ones? When it was time to dust, I was permitted to touch the glass panes--

even the ones that were stenciled around the edges with small delicate lacy snowflakes. Did my father ever place his whole hand upon each pane of color, wishing that he could absorb the pure essence of living light unto himself, hoping that the moment of merger could slake a thirst for something that only the expression *panting after living water* came close to describing?

From the moment I heard that expression in church, I loved to go downtown to the worship service. There, the words read from the Bible washed over me like the light from the colored window, fulfilling my heart's ache for beauty and the truthful expression of it.

Once, Mr. Ashley sat beside me on the brown stairs and asked me what I saw as I stared at the colored light, and I said, "I see music mostly."

And he nodded seriously, and replied solemnly, "I see it too. Not always, and mostly with you, but I see the music too."

The language of beauty had a variety of names. Sometimes it flowed in me as colored light, and sometimes it looked like music, and sometimes--the best times--it was the springing up of words that came out of the thirst for living water and were spoken as prayers that drifted into heaven as smoke from a slow burning fire, passing through the angels themselves, flooding their dear heavenly faces in colored earth lights, and it wasn't so much the substance of the prayer that mattered--it was the faith that caused their creation and which infused them with an energy to exist and soar upward to God, the maker and receiver of beauty's reports.

Oh, Beauty! It called my name early, and whatever form it assumed or demanded be born out of me, I gave myself over to it, marveling that even a small whisper of a prayer like the one I uttered for Mr. Ashley could bear what the Bible calls "fruit." For just like the story of Genesis where God spoke our world into being, we have the words to create. We need only speak and sometimes just whisper the words, dropping them like fruit seeds at the feet of God, and he can either make them grow or not. On Alabama Street, I discovered early that if I could take the time to see the fruit blooming, God seemed more ready to bring to life the visions of my heart.

It was my heart's hope and prayer that Mr. Ashley could take a long walk outside. Soon after our first trip together, he tried. He went slowly, and he didn't invite me for company or as a witness, but I watched him from the other side of the screen door inside the foyer where I was sweeping. I prayed a second time, "God, bring his old bones to life, like the ones from Ezekiel."

Before long, Mr. Ashley was walking a little further. He began by just walking to the next block where he sat on a bench at the bus stop. Buses would come by and stop, and he waved them on, because he wasn't waiting for the bus in order to catch it. He liked to absorb the sight of so many people going places. It made him feel better. I admired that about Mr. Ashley-- he didn't have to be going on a journey himself in order to enjoy the trips others were taking. He was a noble man, who got stronger from the sight of people living lives in motion.

Soon, he was walking all the way to town where he went to a small cafe called The Captain's Table inside Belk Hudson. There, he ate lunch. He told me about it. I had passed by that cafe with my grandmother, who didn't take me inside because they didn't serve beer. Going out to lunch helped him because he was able to do more than remember: he was a part of that motion of a daily life he preferred.

As if coming back from working a long day at the office, he took a taxi cab home in the afternoons, pulling up in front of Alabama Street where I was watching for him while I swept the sidewalk. He saluted me jauntily with two fingers tipped at his brow, as if he were a returning soldier. And I would pretend to sweep faster and faster for him, leading the way up the porch, and he laughed and laughed 'cause he thought I was funny.

Mr. Ashley was much happier after he began taking his walks to town. But he grew less interested in me, though he always spoke to me. I was never invisible to him. And once, when it suddenly occurred to him that he had not offered me a cold drink in a long time, he held out a dime to me apologetically, in a hurry now to be going, and said I could go across the street to the Scott Street grocery store and buy what I wanted, and I said, "No, thank you, sir," *because good girls don't take money from men.*

That day, he and I knew that whatever had been between us for a few months ended with the offer of his dime, and I didn't resent the offer and he wasn't embarrassed by my refusal, because in addition to the understanding that sunlight translated into colors by a special window looks like music and is set in the background of angels singing, he and I also knew that there were seasons between people and ours had come mostly to an end. A natural law got born in me: There are endings and beginnings that exist without requiring the judgment of being good or bad. *The motion of living can be trusted.*

Which didn't mean that I didn't feel sad. Years later, I identified this sadness as grief, but when I was a child, I called it loneliness, and maybe grief more rightly is that. There was this sadness, because his company and his need of me had been a special treat I looked forward to, but I had only to see Mr. Ashley walking off down the street with the sunshine of love on his face to remember that there was nothing to feel sad about really. Sometimes when a man leaves you it is exactly what should happen.

3
The Beauty Room

After my baby brother died, Daddy got busy making his girls a beauty room in our new house on Edgemont Avenue. We needed to move from the apartment building on Alabama Street because we needed to live close enough to walk to school. Mother didn't drive. Bellingrath school was right across the street from our new house, and the room where we all got ready to go anywhere was on the opposite side of the house next to what had been for months the nursery. Our brother's nursery became the guest room again, and the laundry room to which it was connected expanded in its utility to become the beauty room. It's where we did our hair.

Daddy installed a pink sink with grey speckles like they have in real beauty parlors so that my sisters and I could wash each other's hair; and there was a stand-up rolling hair dryer which moved around the room to our various assigned chairs when it was our turn to sit under it. Our names were written in black magic marker underneath our chairs as if the colors alone would not be enough to declare its owner. Mine was a sunny yellow. Mary Ellen's was

Christmas red. Patty's was royal blue. (Daddy called her Princess.) Mother used the small wooden chair with the white cushion that she pulled out of from her sewing machine, and sometimes that was Julie's chair, too. Julie was the baby—a toddler, really.

We kept our hair rollers and jars of Dippety-do in our assigned drawers at the long communal dresser that stretched the width of the wall nearest the window. It had a big mirror, too, and there was plenty of space for cans of hairspray and rolling tissue papers that we used to ensure our hair dried evenly by being blotted and rolled securely around this paper. These little slips of paper poked out of our rollers which then often fit snugly inside hairnets that held the rollers in place.

The only real problem we ever had in the beauty room was running out of hot water, and often the laundry waited until the rituals of baths and shampooing of five heads of hair had been completed. Then, the first load of towels would be washed. The never-ending cycle of laundry kept us company in the beauty room while we dried our hair or did our nails while we watched our mother and daddy come back to life "After we lost the boy."

What Makes a Man a Hero?

That phrase lingered in the air for a long time, as my sisters and I tried to make it up to our parents that their hearts had been broken, and they tried to make it up to us that we had lost a brother. Our mother got busy doing odd jobs around the house—that's what she called them. And they were odd. She painted the originally yellow kitchen clock black and the grout around the tile was painted a glossy black, too.

That's when Daddy took on the creation of the beauty room, his offering to us during this season of confusion and sadness. "I'm outnumbered," he'd laughingly explain when the room was shown off to a neighbor or one of mama's sisters, who laughed too because they were supposed to follow his lead.

Almost everybody saw through him, I think, but no one would say out loud that the beauty room was not only a consolation to us—beauty for ashes-- but an apology from dad lest we think at any level that he had really wanted that boy more than he would have wanted a girl. Or all his girls.

"I'm blessed," he would announce suddenly, jarringly. "We're blessed to have each other to love." And heads would nod—rolled heads as we checked each other's reflections in the mirror keeping the secret that mother was deeply silent and distant, and daddy wasn't himself-- not yet.

Dad imitated himself the way he once had been, and we performed for him in the beauty room, a theater of sorts where we girls played out the parts assigned to us after we lost the boy. We washed our hair in his special sink and we rolled our hair for him, enjoying the dresser and our drawers and our personalized chairs. We listened to the "Beatles" and to Mary Ellen, the oldest and our lead singer, offer commentary about aspects of romance celebrated in pop hits. "That lyric undermines the intention of the song, doesn't it? You're listening, aren't you?"

"To 'Can't Buy Me Love.' Yes. I think you're right." I always agreed with whatever Mary Ellen's viewpoint was. She was the family genius.

Patty, the family princess, would only watch us --her two older sisters-- and tilt her head sideways, studying us. "Maybe," she said, a thoughtful assessing answer that previewed psychology would become her field of inquiry.

A lover of music, Julie, the baby of the family, danced in the way that a toddler moves to music.

Daddy would come by during our Saturday evenings in the beauty room and watch us wash and roll and dance with each other and start the laundry and stay together as the loads of laundry dried and then were folded on the big table that flanked the other end of the room.

Most nights we weren't dancing for fun; we were dancing to convince him that we were happy too and that life was as pretty as a beauty room could make it. Daddy wanted to give us that assurance in the beauty room; we tried to give it right back.

Occasionally while his girls folded the clothes, separating them into the stacks to be distributed to separate bedrooms, tears sprang to his eyes, and he pretended they didn't. We pretended not to see.

Each week, after he left to take his bath and before he laid himself down to sleep earlier than the rest of us, one of us stealthily kidnapped his Sunday shoes from his bedroom closet. We took turns polishing his shoes for church. We washed his dress shirts and ironed them. We made sure that he had a clean white handkerchief in his pocket for church. We took care of him in our way. He took care of us and mama in his.

Then, the girl whose turn it was to polish the shoes, returned them, moving stealthily like a burglar into his bedroom while he snored gently, a comforting sound that all was well. Then, pressing ever so slightly with her fingertips she pushed the sliding wooden door of the closet back enough to place the shoes inside on the floor underneath his church-going suit that hung above. Then, she'd leave the door just a little bit ajar so that the lingering aroma of that black shoe polish would not cling to his good Sunday clothes.

Back in the beauty room, the drawers would be closed and all the papers put away—the music turned off as soon as Daddy had gone off to bed. The chairs were pushed back against the wall and the folded towels and underwear picked up to be carried to separate bedrooms. Wordlessly Mary Ellen switched off the radio while Patty prepared the coffee pot for the next day. Julie hurried to her side of the bed in the pink bedroom she shared with Mary Ellen.

Patty and I shared the blue one. Then in the night, with Daddy sleeping and mother solemnly working her crossword puzzle in the kitchen, Mary Ellen often sang a song for us.

She had a pure and beautiful voice that sounded to me like an angel singing in the next room. Her nightly lullaby was a constant reminder that beauty was doing its work, and over time, it did.

4
Legacy of a Very Handy Man

As I pedaled off on my bicycle to the post office, my daddy, who had just pumped up my tires with his own air compressor, called after me, "I hope you don't break down between here and there!"

It is just a two-mile ride to the post office, but no matter the distance I'm traveling or the current circumstances, that pessimistic parting shot is always my daddy's idea of a proper farewell: a doomsday good-bye. I can almost hear him praying behind my back whenever I leave him: "Lord, be merciful to that girl. There's no telling what could happen to her out there."

Dad's attitude is based on seventeen years of working the midnight shift as a troubleshooter for the local air-force base. Before that, he managed an apartment building. He also sold insurance. His work experience added up to a solid belief that the worst often happens, and he devoted his life as a father to preparing his four daughters for the various afflictions and plagues, he either remembers or can imagine.

They are considerable.

At age eleven, my oldest sister, Mary Ellen, was issued a small hatchet. She was in charge of it. It went under her side of the bed. Its purpose? To chop a hole through the bedroom window if the house caught on fire during the night and Dad wasn't there and Mom couldn't get to us. Mom had her own hatchet.

Dad's idea of a useful Christmas present one year was to give us girls each a can of shaving cream and a new safety razor. Another time, he gave us billfolds containing different-sized screwdrivers. No sexist, the next year he gave us portable sewing kits.

In our thirties now and having been exposed to most of Dad's survival sermonettes more than a few times, we are subjected to a subtle test-taking. Dad does it very cagily, but the underlying question is always the same: Are his girls going to prove to be good Boy Scouts—always prepared for the nasty surprises that life has to offer? By our preparedness we will justify his life's work as a father.

At the annual lighting of my furnace, on the very day before cold weather is predicted, Dad shows up early in the morning, refuses my stall of an offer of freshly brewed coffee, and asks me, "Where are your matches, your flashlight, and a nine-inch candle?"

Like a nurse assisting in surgery, I pull these items from a drawer next to the room where he'll be working.

Dad smiles. He is a fulfilled father in that moment. But the glow doesn't last.

The door to the heating unit sticks. "When's the last time you oiled these hinges?"

The question feels accusatory. I shrug and answer him with a question. "Last year? About this time?" I'm not into hinges.

"WD-40," he demands, shaking his head. I'm off to the kitchen, where I find my can of WD-40 hiding underneath the sink, camouflaged by a pile of old rags. I leave the door ajar, hoping that Dad will spy those old rags—he loves them so.

"I don't suppose you have the straw that comes with it," he says, his voice changing. He is preparing to be disappointed. "It helps to aim the lubricant if you have that straw."

Smugly, I fondle the tiny plastic straw, pulling it gently free from the inch of tape I've used to secure it to the can. Our eyes meet, and he nods approvingly. It is a sweet moment of pleasing a parent.

For there are many times when I feel like a disappointment as a daughter not to have exercised more of what I have learned from Dad. Living next door to him, I find it temptingly easy to call him up for favors rather than do a job myself. It's not like I don't know what to do. I have been listening to his survival lessons for over thirty years now, and I can prove it.

Here are a few of Dad's tips, just as he told them to me.

Always open the nozzle of a garden hose again to relieve the pressure after turning off the faucet. The water pressure can build up from a residual drip and burst your hose.

Carry a jug of water in the car. You never know when you'll break down on the road. A person can live for days without food, but for only seventy-two hours without water.

If you smell escaping gas in a room, open the window immediately and unplug the telephone. A spark from a ringing telephone can set off a gas fire.

There's hardly anything in the world that doesn't work better if you put a little grease on it. It's grease, not love, that makes the world go around.

In addition to the litany of survival rules, Dad offered this standard advice for gift-giving: "Honey, when you need to buy a present for a man for his birthday or any other occasion, don't buy him a shirt or a tie. Show him you've got some sense. Go to the hardware store and buy him a big roll of silver duct tape. There's not a man alive who doesn't want a big role of that."

5
Barking Dogs & Dead Peacocks

Mr. Weir's peacocks killed themselves, flying furiously up into the cage overhead because, claimed Old Man Weir, my father's dogs charged up to the fence and barked at them.

Taking Old Man Weir's word for it that peacocks cannot stand dogs barking, Dad behaved as a good neighbor, took responsibility for the loss, paid Mr. Weir for the dead birds, and had an electric fence installed to shock some sense-or at least some distance--into his four dogs.

Mr. Weir took my daddy's money, promptly gave up raising peacocks, and is now, much to my father's stupefaction, raising dogs. Fancy dogs. Competition dogs. Dogs with bushy hair and aristocratic noses. The kind of dog, Old Man Weir says, that does not bark. "I've trained my dogs not to bark, and if they ever start barking when I don't want them to, well, I just look at them, and they always shut right up."

I can't look at Old Man Weir when he says this, because it's such an outright lie. I ride on my bicycle every day past his house which he has named The Golden

Nugget Ranch on my way to the post office, and his dog barks a blue streak at me. I bark right back. It's a harmless show of rebellion that leaves me hoarse.

Frankly, I don't know how Mr. Weir could possibly not hear that old dog and me having our daily barking match. I'd think he was deaf if I didn't know of his many mean-spirited plans reported to me by my nephew, Matthew, who keeps me up on all the neighborhood news.

"The lady down the street told Old Man Weir that if Pa races Luke in his car, (Matt's black Labrador retriever) down her road one time too many and runs over her Chihuahua, she's gonna sue Pa for thousands and thousands of dollars."

Because our Pa does not like to chain up his dogs, he has to race Luke the Lab in his gold-colored Cadillac to get out of our neighborhood. This means he goes past the Chihuahua's house twice before Luke finally runs out of steam and goes home.

"I've come to a complete stop to let that pitiful-looking mutt cross the road," my father says, defending himself.

"Mr. Weir says that the policeman, who lives at the bottom of the hill, is waiting for you with the radar gun, Pa, and he's gonna catch you racing Luke down the road and give you a speeding ticket," Matt reported.

Now, this makes my daddy mad. He

happens to be that policeman's mortgagor, and the man does not make his house payments on time. The policeman doesn't like my daddy dunning him for the money, and so he wants to get some of his own pride back by giving our Pa an expensive speeding ticket.

"Forewarned is forearmed," my daddy commented, tight-lipped.

I could see him reflecting on how he has *bent over backwards* to try and please that policeman and his weepy wife, who bought the house and who have complained from day one about everything from the size of the handles on the kitchen cabinets to an elusive and peculiar smell in the bathtub.

"I told you not to sell that house to those people," my mother reminds him. She did tell him that. I heard her. Daddy doesn't listen to mother when she hauls out her intuition. He likes to do people favors, and he knew up front that the policeman didn't have much money, because his wife has been in a car accident and all their ready cash was tied up in paying hospital bills.

Dad always makes the same good-hearted mistake. He thinks, *Boy, if I were in that kind of shape I'd sure like someone to help me.* He doesn't understand that people often resent their neighbors and their landlords--no matter how hard they try to get along.

"Mr. Weir says that when the policeman catches you and gives you that ticket, he wants to be there to see it happen."

"Well, that really gets my goat," my father exclaims. "All I have ever done is try and please that old man. But I'll be doggoned if I'm going to go on being nice to a man who wants to watch me get in trouble with the police."

There are some people you can't be nice to. They see it as a sign of weakness and take advantage of you. Women know this their whole lives. After turning the cheek a few times, Christians eventually accept the axiom but keep turning their cheeks anyway. Good neighbors learn it the hard way.

Mr. Weir thinks kindness to animals and to other people is a sign of weakness. He's been known to set traps to catch small animals, and then he keeps them in cages that are so small they can't turn around. I've heard him speak crossly to his wife, and he brazenly lies that his dogs never bark.

In contrast to him, our Pa has been known to walk around the neighborhood at lunch time and fill the water bowls of animals whose owners work during the day. Before our Pa goes to bed each night, he opens the back door and sings out to his dogs, "Y'all go to sleep now. Lord willing, we'll see each other tomorrow."

Now, Pa has reluctantly bought a chain for Luke and laments that he must tie up his dog whenever he wants to drive away from the house. "I just live back here on this piece of swamp land with my dogs. I almost never even talk to anyone. I don't understand why anyone would want to see something bad happen to me."

There is a reason, but I'm not gonna be the one to tell him.

Dad may be an animal lover and he tries to be a good neighbor, but he falls short in one serious category. He is also a kind of criminal--a dognapper, a well as a speed demon. Matthew's dog Luke prefers to live with Pa, and he isn't the only dog from the neighborhood to desert its owner for my dad's brand of room and board.

Spot, Big Shot, and the Incredible Hulk all left neighborhood owners to move in with Dad. These neighbors, who have felt the public shame of being rejected by their animals, have very long memories.

"When the policeman catches up with his house payments, maybe you can let Luke run free again," Matthew suggests. It is an enlightened response--a mature suggestion from such a young boy.

As my gesture of consolation, I bought our Pa a tee-shirt that reads: **If You Can't Run With The Big Dogs You Better**

Stay On The Porch. "Wear it when you drive by that Chihuahua's house," I encouraged him.

So far, Pa hasn't responded well to this situation. He's taken this business of barking dogs and dead peacocks pretty much to heart. I can hardly stand to see him grieve so--to see him chain Luke and get in his Cadillac and drive off sedately, lonely--a man without his dog.

He has gone into a kind of mourning that the world isn't what he thought it was or should be. Since all this has happened, he has just about quit checking the water bowls of neighborhood dogs. He's decided that it is courting trouble. Now, he just carries a ten-pound bag of Purina Dog Chow in his back seat in order to feed the pitiful stray dogs out on the highway, who look as if they haven't had a square meal in a long time.

Other than peacocks dying and dogs barking, my own days have stayed pretty much the same. Outside, Mr. Weir's dog is patrolling the common fence by the creek. He barks the same blue streak whenever I go by his house, and Mr. Weir never seems to hear his animal make the sounds he claims do not exist.

Every day on my way to the mail box, I yell as loudly as I can, "Shut up, you loud-barking, blue-haired, worrisome mutt!"

Maybe God will forgive me for taking my anger for mean neighbors out on this blue-blooded, show-off dog. But, shoot, if I'd been a peacock, I'd be dead by now.

6
Joy Ride with the Boys

"I told my brother Tommy that I wasn't ever getting in the car with him again to go anywhere unless we have an agreement, and I mean we're all going to sign it, that there will be a break every four hours for food and other resting purposes."

"Are you telling me that he wouldn't let you go to the bathroom?"

"I'm telling you that I was close to hysterics by the time we got home. I lived off pretzels for eight hours. Pretzels!"

"No food at all?"

My mother shook her head of golden-brown curls vigorously.

Well, I think she was shaking her head. She was still quivering from spending seventeen hours in the car with two men who had competed to see how long each one could last in the car before the other would cry, "Enough! You win! I need to rest."

"If we hadn't needed to buy two tanks of gas, I never would have gotten to stretch my legs. The second time we stopped at a Texaco station, I raced in the bathroom so I could get to the snack aisle of the food mart and buy myself a package of peanut butter crackers. I had it all planned: I was going to sit in the car and smack real loud and not offer either one of them as much as a crumb, but Tommy slipped up on me at the cash register and grabbed my arm and said, "Now, you don't want to buy any of that junk food. Jerry and I are going to get you a good meal just as soon as we see a place that looks right.'"

The trouble is, no place ever looks right to my mother's brother Tommy and her husband Jerry, my Daddy, when they're on a car trip together.

"It's like they get mesmerized by the road, and it won't let them go." Mother said. Some memory of forgotten knowledge crosses her face, and she stifled a shudder. "Once he gets behind that wheel, it's as if he can't get out again until we reach the destination or run out of gas. Like he's possessed or something."

Her left eye twitching, she placed a hand on her quivering muscle and said, "You know, it took us only fifteen hours to get there and seventeen hours to come back."

After you already knew the way?" I asked. "How come it took longer to get home?"

Her whole body convulsed in response. She didn't trust herself to speak.

"It wasn't me!" Daddy piped up, taking advantage of the opportunity to defend himself. "I was willing to stop the car at any time."

He'd been listening to everything Mother said about Tommy and him, but was not dismayed by the picture she painted. The members of my family freely engage in this kind of open criticism of one another's behavior. It's how we keep from killing each other.

Right now, my father is pleading innocent. And oh, he looks innocent. Perfectly relaxed. Not a twitch in him. But he's just as bad as his brother-in-law. He thinks that I don't remember family vacations when we girls didn't dare mention the word *bathroom* when on a car trip. I don't know what it is about men, but they don't consider a bathroom break a legitimate reason to stop the car when on a road trip.

Mother goes wild-eyed when she hears Daddy's claim. She grips her chair to keep from putting her hands around his neck to choke a confession out of him.

I know how she feels. I've ridden to town and back and been driven wild-eyed by the road guide speech Dad gives when riding in the car while I am driving.

Just this morning, we went to town, and he said to me during the twenty minute ride: "Boy, did you see that dead possum? Hardly ever see a possum alive. Possums....they just have a terrible time. I remember going hunting with Old Man Jackson. He had a cabin in the woods. He trapped a possum in a cage that wasn't big enough to hold a squirrel. Jackson opened the cage and the critter could barely crawl out. He headed straight toward the woods.

"Then, Jackson shot him. Used him for target practice. Killed him dead. I wouldn't have anything else to do with a man who treated a possum like that. Probably a special place in hell for him.

"Wow! Didn't you see that bump? You took that bump pretty hard and fast. I'd watch that bump the next time you come this way. You could knock a tire loose. Worse still, you could get your whole front end out of alignment. Truth is, if you take a bump like that too fast, you'll knock the front end right off the car, and then where would you be? Do you drive like this when I'm not in the car with you?"

I didn't try to answer my father's questions. I'm not sure how I drive when he isn't in the car with me. I know that I barely notice dead possums and bumps in the road. I am haunted in that moment by another question, however: *If a tree falls in the woods, does it make a sound?* Rephrased, *Do men stop the car, ask for directions when lost, or ignore the sight of a fallen possum when they're alone in a car?*

My father is unaware that my mind has taken a detour.

"It seems to me that the other bumps in the road have sunk in below street level. Now we have sink holes in public roads. Sink holes are just as bad on your car as a bump like the one you just took too fast. You could catch the side of the tire and cut the rubber, whammo, bam, skid. The tire could blow. Your car would swerve off the road and hit anything, and you'd be dead. Someone coming along behind you might run smack-dab into you. We'd all end up like that possum on the road back there."

I was beginning to think that a possum's end is a merciful one. I told my mother about the ride after she finished telling me some more about her trip with the two men she calls boys.

"I hear what you're saying. The two of them talked like that for seventeen hours. If I hadn't been so hungry, I might have listened to them, and if I had they certainly would have driven me crazy."

My mother didn't look particularly sane, but I didn't tell her that. Time would give her ease.

She was near the refrigerator now, the bathroom, and that proximity alone would bring comfort. However, I did recommend that she write that travel contract out while she still had the details on her mind about what makes a comfortable joyride and what does not.

And then before she goes anywhere with them again and that includes church, my mama needs to get both those boys to sign it.

7
Secret Agent Man

Whenever one of the cable channels runs a pair of James Bond movies on the same night, my parents hightail it thirty miles up the road to their favorite Clanton motel and check in for the night. I picture them riding down the Interstate with Dad practicing how he will introduce himself to the registration clerk; "Hello. I'm Bond. James Bond."

For both my parents there is something about watching 007 that inspires them to cut loose from the everyday world of family frictions and check themselves in as double-ought adventurers.

I heard them describe their great escape routine to my Uncle Tommy, a 70-year-old newlywed who is still exploring honeymoon ideas with his new bride. My father has the reputation of being a honeymoon expert because of these James Bond trips he and mother take.

"The way we work it, Shorty stays in the car while I register for the room. Then, Shorty gets the ice while I set the thermostat to working. While she fixes our glasses, tunes in the right channel on the television, I open the Vienna sausages and pop the top on a fresh 2-liter bottle of the Real Thing. I don't mean that new Coke they came up with. I'm talking honest-to-goodness Coca-Cola. A fresh Coca-Cola never tastes so good as when you're propped on a motel bed with clean sheets underneath you and a box of fresh Ritz crackers nearby. When we get ready for some real food, we order up a plate of fried chicken delivered right to the room. Women love Room Service. If she wants a pot of coffee, I order that too. Even if there's a coffeemaker in the room. Women set a high value on having a pot of coffee come to the room. Don't even ask questions about it. In the long run, it's the best two dollars and a half you will ever spend."

I heard my Uncle Tommy's voice grow low at this point, and I could not discern the question he asked but I heard my father's answer.

"Oh, no. We prefer a room in the back of the motel so we can watch the parking lot. You have no idea how much activity goes on in a motel parking lot at night. Sometimes, after we've watched all the Bond movies, we just sit back and watch the trucks and cars. It goes on all night long. It can get pretty exciting."

Mother piped up. "And, we answer the telephone, because even where nobody in town knows us, someone still calls us up."

It is mother's obligation to mention the ringing telephone, because in the past when they checked in to the motel for a night of James Bond, a woman checked out Dad while he was registering. Because mother was waiting in the car, the woman assumed Dad was a Gentleman Alone. She discovered his room number, and before he had the safety lock turned on the door, she dialed him up, and asked if he wanted some company.

Unlike his hero, Bond, who gets propositioned by mysterious dangerous women all the time, Dad panicked. He slammed the phone down and asked Mother to double-check the door.

That's what really happened-- Mother told me. But it's not the way Dad describes the incident to others, especially his brother-in-law, Tommy, the newlywed, who looks up to my father.

Dad tells the story this way: "I never even noticed the woman, but she must have seen me, and that was all it took. She couldn't help herself; she had to call."

"I answer the phone in the motel now," Mother interrupts. "And believe me, it rings. We went down there last week to watch **Thunderball** and **Goldfinger**. He was almost asleep when the phone rang. This time, someone had called in a bomb threat, and all the motel rooms had to be evacuated."

"I knew the call was important because Shorty's voice gets steady and calm when the news is serious. I did just what she told me to do. We got dressed in the middle of the night, and then we stayed out in our car in the parking lot until the time the bomb was supposed to explode. After it didn't go off, we went back to bed."

"You could sleep after all that?" Tommy asked, incredulously.

"Sure," they replied in unison.

"We always sleep good in a motel, especially after we've watched a James Bond double feature," Mother added.

"It's because we can," Dad added. "Shorty takes care of the telephone, and when trouble hits, like a bomb threat, it's not like I'm expected to keep it from blowing up."

Mother nodded happily. "That's right. We always have a good time on James Bond night at that motel. It's very exciting."

8
Two Shakes of a Lamb's Tail

It was rib-eye steak night at my sister Mary Ellen's house, and I could tell before the Worcestershire sauce ever made it to me that Mama had something on her mind.

Finally, right after the baked potatoes had been passed out and the butter and sour cream were making the rounds, Mother cupped her hands formally in front of her as if to ask the blessing; but instead, she accused one of her daughters of being a bowl thief.

"I hate to have to say this. I really do," she began, sweeping our faces with that penetrating brown-eyed gaze. "But I have a deluxe Tupperware serving bowl with a snap lock lid, and I can't find it anywhere."

Daddy interrupted Mother. "There'll be no questions asked," he assured us. "I'm sure one of you girls just borrowed the bowl and forgot to tell your mother. But she's going on a trip with her girlfriends next week, and she needs her bowl."

"They know I am responsible for bringing the spinach dip." Mother said, and her tone was less prayerful.

This offense committed against her was more than simple theft. Her honor as the spinach dip queen was in question if she did not have the perfect bowl to carry it in, and the fact that one of her own children would put her reputation in such jeopardy was on par in her mind with what King Lear's viperish girls did to their parent.

The room fell silent as we supposedly contemplated our consciences, but this awkward silence was soon broken by my nephew, Matthew, who obviously sympathized with mother's plight but did not understand the implications inherent in the alleged crime. He only knew that someone else had lost something, and he had, too.

"Talk about things disappearing," Matthew said. "I cannot find my sheep's tail. I have looked all over the backyard for it.

Matthew belongs to the Future Farmers of America and is raising a sheep as a project.

"I thought you wanted your sheep's tail to fall off," Dad remarked. "What was it I heard about your putting that special rubber band on the tail to cut off the circulation so that it would fall off?"

Matthew nodded yes, vigorously. "That's right. I did that. You remember."

He is young and does not yet understand that remembering something before it disappeared is not the same thing as coming up with a clue that will aid in finding it.

I felt sorry for Matt, so I added a two-cent memory. "I saw your sheep and his tail a few days ago. That tail was hanging straight down the back of your animal, and it didn't sway one iota. It looked like a dead tail to me."

"The tail is supposed to die and fall off. And it should be out in the back yard somewhere, but I can't find it."

"Your sheep probably buried his tail after it fell off. You will never find it," Mother said, impatiently dismissing her grandson's problem. She was intent on solving her own. "What I want to know is, where is my spinach dip bowl?"

None of us would look Mother in the eye when she asked that question. I don't know why my sisters couldn't face her, but I could not look at Mother because my biscuit-making bowl has been missing for a long time, and I figured that she might have it. I'm loath to accuse my mother or any of my sisters of being a bowl thief, because I was raised to believe that stealing a woman's favorite bowl is akin to borrowing her last pair of designer panty hose without permission or using her lipstick that she has just managed to make match the shape of her lips. It's not exactly a sin, but it's a bad thing to do.

"I just think it's curious that one day I have something and the next day I don't," Mother summed up bitterly.

At last, she picked up her steak knife and began to saw through her piece of meat. It was cold, and the cutting was tough work. Determined, she kept at it. By then, none of us had much of an appetite, and we fiddled with our salads.

Something in Mother's tone triggered a gallant impulse in Dad, who stopped altogether being our protective father, and once again assumed his position as Mother's hero.

"This reminds me of those days when all of you girls still lived at home, and I could never find my scissors or my Scotch tape or the glue. When I asked any of you where something was no one had ever seen it." Just remembering the good old days made Dad bitter. "Those things didn't just walk off by themselves, and neither did your mother's bowl."

"There is another solution to the mystery of things disappearing," I offered tentatively. "Is it possible that one of us has multiple personality disorder?"

They didn't know what I meant at first, so I explained. "I am reading this book where the main character gets kidnapped as a little girl and is abused and because the stress is so awful, her personality splits off into different people. Later in life, one of those split-off parts of her gets accused of murdering her English teacher, and her own sister thinks she could have done it. The girl can't defend herself because she has no conscious memory of what the other personalities do."

"I thought when you outgrew Nancy Drew, we wouldn't have to listen to any more plot summaries from books at the dinner table," my oldest sister complained. She was the hostess for our family supper, and it wasn't going well. She had decided to blame me.

"None of you girls was ever kidnapped," Mother interjected, sounding regretful. "Furthermore, none of my girls would dare to have multiple personalities. I wouldn't permit that. One personality is enough for any well-bred person."

"The only reason I am bringing this up is that the other day I was trying to gather my income tax information, and I went to find my record of contributions to the church where I know I put it, and my tax document was gone."

"That happens to me every year," Dad said. "I call myself putting all the receipts in one place; but when I go to look for them, they are not all there." His gaze swept us again—a foreign look in his eye that didn't seem like our daddy at all.

"I don't guess it's likely that two people in the same family would have multiple personality disorder," I conceded. "There must be another explanation." I studied my sisters to see if I could tell whether they were hiding some other kinds of mischievous, secret women behind their eyes.

Reading my mind, they faced me unashamed, unafraid of what I might see. Actually, I was the first to look away.

When I did, my nephew announced, looking right at me: "There's your bowl thief right there."

"I did not take my mother's bowl," I denied, shocked by my nephew's accusation. "I have my own bowls. I have two Tupperware bowls with snap lock lids. I don't need to steal anyone's bowl."

"What color are your bowls?" Mother asked softly. Her brown-eyed gaze pierced me.

"What color was yours?" I asked, drawing back.

"You first," she ordered.

"One bowl is red, and the other bowl is yellow."

She chewed a small bite of cold steak slowly, then swallowed.

"My bowl is yellow. When did you buy your so-called yellow bowl?"

I had no memory of making the purchase, and I could not explain why I would have brought two bowls of different colors.

The silence was unbearable. I broke it. "The yellow Tupperware bowl is mine, but you are welcome to have it."

"I guess I am," Mother said, settling back.

"See there," Daddy said. "I told you we'd find your bowl."

I could feel some inner part of my personality attempting to split off as I was falsely accused of a crime I had not committed. My own mother was stealing my bowl, and my father was backing her up.

While my family drifted into a lighter conversation, I, abused, maligned, robbed of my yellow bowl and my biscuit-making bowl, took the higher road of martyred silence and, holding tightly onto my identity by keeping a firm grip on my knife and fork, resolved to finish my dinner nobly, heroically, as if I had nothing to hide. This course of action was not easy, considering the intense, accusing, as yet unasked questions about a missing sheep's tail still lurking in my young nephew's innocent eyes.

9
Baby Toss

Every now and then, my father takes off his baseball cap and tosses it at his newest grandchild, Katie. This time, his cap crests Katie's small round head and falls inside her play pen, which sits in the corner of my parents' large living room.

Katie laughs, adores the game. Pa is disconcerted though. He is losing his touch. The cap is meant to find its mark--that is, Katie's head--and stay there.

"I cannot believe you are playing ring-toss using the baby's head as your target."

Pa is startled at the critical edge to my voice. "It likes it."

"She," I correct him. Babies are Its to Dad until they are old enough to choose a public rest room.

Dad leans over the play pen, retrieves the blue cap, nuzzles her neck, and pretends to have trouble standing upright again. While he is bent over at the waist, Katie pulls that lock of thin gray hair that my father combs from the back of his head to the front to cover his bald space, and she yanks it hard. It is a wiry stretch of hair that we have tried curling, spraying, and fussing at to make it behave. But like the man it belongs to, the hair is unmanageable.

As his lock of hair rises slowly, defying gravity, Pa straightens, and Katie cries out. To placate her, Pa bends again, scoops her up first to his waist, next to his shoulder. Her arms flail; she hangs onto his hair for support.

I catch my breath. It is just a question of time before....

"The kid isn't afraid of anything," Dad assesses proudly.

The kid is his current favorite granddaughter, who he and my mother babysit five days a week for ten hours each day. "And, it likes people. Never meets a stranger."

"Yes, Katie is sociable," I concur.

Dad adds, deciding to acknowledge Katie's girl-ness: "The more people looking at her and talking to her, the better she likes it."

Making airplane sounds, he lowers Katie back to his waist and settles her into the crook of his elbow. "I was thinking we ought to buy some of those store mannequins and sit them around the room so she could have plenty of company."

I check to see if he is joking. He is not.

"Don't you think that she would figure out the difference before too long?" I ask dryly.

He doesn't hear me.

"Only I don't know where to buy mannequins."

He takes Katie to the couch, where she sits on his belly and pulls at his belt buckle.

"Katie," I whisper. I hold out my arms hopefully. I shake a rattle at her. She only has eyes for Pa.

Dad takes the rattle from me and says, "Look here. This is a new trick I've taught her." He taps the rattle on Katie's forehead to make her eyes blink. He taps and taps--she blinks and blinks.

"Stop that!" I demand.

"It likes it" he teases. He has used the word *It* this time to provoke me, and it worked. I feel provoked.

"Well, her mother wouldn't like it."

Dad shrugs and stops. "Those girls don't know how to have a good time," he says to Katie, as if she isn't one of us.

I reach out again, but Katie takes one long look at me, her aunt, and lets her eyes glaze over. As long as her grandfather is near, she isn't going anywhere else. He is her preferred person. No amount of what may look like abuse changes that.

Pa pulls Katie up to his face and croons something like, "Sit, Spot, sit."

"You treat that baby as if she's a dog," I snip.

"I love dogs," he says, missing my

point. "Besides, this little thing has driven Spot crazy. He's so jealous of her."

"Your dog, Spot, was crazy before this baby ever got here."

Katie reaches out and grabs Pa's nose. She pulls on it for a while. She reaches for his glasses. She gnaws on a shoulder bone. Dad is perfectly free with himself. Katie can attack any part of him.

He wrestles with her in a way that reminds me of his lying on the grass outside while three dogs pounce on him. He buries his head against her stomach and growls. She slaps him on the back of his head and pulls on his hair some more. She is the only person in the family that he lets near that last special lock of hair--his last few strands.

"You aren't getting too rough with her, are you?"

"She started it."

"I see," I say.

I do not add that it wouldn't be the way that I would play with her. I've never seen a woman play with a baby the way a man does. Ring toss, baby toss, growl and yank. These rough and tumble games aren't recommended in the books on child care that I read, and frankly, I don't know why not. Dad is right. The kid eats it up.

10
Safe at Home

"I wish you wouldn't bathe the baby in the sink when it's threatening to rain," my father said.

"Where do you think I should bathe her?" my sister Patty asked.

"Why bathe her at all? How dirty could she be? It's not like she works for a living," Dad opined.

"I'm going to bathe the baby," Patty stated flatly. "I promise I won't use up the hot water."

"It's not the hot water I'm worried about. I'm afraid the baby will be struck by lightning."

"Inside the house? In the sink? Before it even starts to rain?"

Dad shrugged off the implicit criticism. "It could happen. Water attracts lightning."

"I'll put my body between the window and Katie," the daughter this man used to call Princess promised. "If lightning strikes, it will hit me first."

That thought seemed to comfort my father temporarily; but after a moment, he argued, "But your hands will be wet, and you'll be holding my Precious Love."

"I promise that my body will absorb

most of the electricity," Patty said, gamely turning on the faucet.

Seeing that the baby was going to be bathed over his protestations, Dad suggested, "Well, at least stand on the rug. It has a rubber bottom. Maybe that will help."

This conversation is typical of the child care discussions that take place around the newest grandchild.

Katie has brought out all of my father's nervousness about the pitfalls of baby-raising, and these parental caveats range from how to bathe Katie to taking the child to the mall, where, in her stroller, this innocent victim, according to my father's view, is forced to breathe dust kicked up by shoppers.

"Why do you want to put a perfectly clean baby in the path of people and their miserable dirty feet?" Dad asked when Patty and Katie headed off to the mall last Saturday.

"We have to go somewhere," my sister said.

"Why?"

"Because the baby can't just stay here all the time."

"Why?"

"Because she finds other people interesting."

"Why?"

"I don't know why she likes other

people. Katie is a social child. She likes to mingle."

"I think you're speaking for yourself and projecting onto the baby," my father theorized, stroking his chin thoughtfully.

Dad has picked up the word projecting from one of the talk shows. Dad's only previous experience with projecting has been the old-fashioned kind, when he showed those home movies of my three sisters and me waving, though we were never really going anywhere.

My sister stifles a comeback, for she has studied psychology, and she knows what's happening here. Our Pa is an anxious grandfather, obsessively cautious about the child he has dubbed Precious Love

After the bath, Patty pushed the baby off in the stroller for a turn in the park. Our Pa stood at the window and watched his Princess and his Precious Love leave the safety of his fortress. His was a somber farewell speech: "I can't believe a child of mine would be fool enough to take the baby to the park. Think of the stray dogs that could be prowling, the squirrels that could be rabid, strangers with germs on their hands touching the swings that the baby will hold, and then she'll put her hands in her mouth. Not to mention all that dirt. God, please help her."

Daddy prays out loud to God, who He

knows always hears him. He thinks we don't.

"Katie will be fine," I promised him.

He looked at me with a fresh suspicion. "Sometimes, I don't know what to make of your sister."

I did. And being her sister, I attempted to deflect some of our father's anxiety from her to me. I confessed softly, "I took Katie to the grocery store this morning."

Before he could launch into his warnings about the dangers lurking at Foodworld, lightning flashed across the sky and jagged threateningly toward the Village Green. Thunder boomed. The neighborhood dogs began to howl. In my mind, I saw them gather, those wild, howling potentially rabid beasts, head off in a stormy herd to the park, where they would attack and devour the innocent children playing there. Or, maybe this time our Precious Love would be struck by lightning.

I had meant to comfort my father-- perhaps in time, to reason with him. Instead, I took my place beside him at the front door, and together we watched for the children to come home.

11
Observe the Man

We pulled over in the car a distance away from the man who sells bird houses and wooden trellises on the side of the road across from our grocery store.

"Let's buy a bird house," Katie says. She automatically assumes that we are shopping. We do shop a great deal, but we aren't this time. We are only looking at the man.

We have looked at a couple of men lately. We contemplated Mel Gibson on the cover of a video box, *Lethal Weapon*. "This is what a good-looking man looks like," I explained simply.

"I know," she said.

I wordlessly pointed out a Mustang convertible and then asked her what she thought.

"Are you saying that I should date men with cars like that?" she asked.

"Not exactly," I replied, wincing.

"You can date a man who drives a Mustang, but you wouldn't date a man because he drives a Mustang, especially if he calls himself Mustang instead of by his name."

"I like the name Mustang," she replied, filing away the idea.

"You would also want to be careful about dating a bald-headed man who drives a convertible in the summertime."

My niece waited for me to explain.

"His head would get sunburned, and he would care less about that than the idea of himself being seen driving in a convertible. It's a kind of thinking that is dangerous."

"Kind of like short men who get a pilot's licenses in order to fly planes to be taller."

"That's right," I concurred, glad that she remembered an earlier lesson.

"And today we're looking at something even more mysterious."

"The man with the bird houses."

We studied him together. He sat on the tail end of a pick-up truck surrounded by the simplest kind of birdhouse. They weren't fancy, intricately carved, or humorously painted. Beside the truck nestled fan-shaped wooden trellises. The inventory never seemed to go down, and he was there every week day, rain or shine.

"Do you suppose he sells a lot of bird houses?" she asked, sensibly, I thought.

"I do not know. I have only rarely seen anyone stop to buy one."

"I wonder what they cost," she added. "Where's the sign with the price?"

"I have never seen a sign with a price."

"I guess you have to stop and ask him."

I nodded succinctly.

"Notice anything else?"

It is the same question I had asked my class of business students when we discussed the dynamics of salesmanship.

"There isn't anything else. He's just sitting there."

I smiled.

"What else should he be doing?"

She observed the man. "Reading a book?"

"Possibly."

"Eating lunch?"

I shrugged. "If he's hungry."

She studied him.

"Where do you think the bird houses come from?" I prodded.

Before I could answer, she provided a theory of her own. "He makes them."

"Does he?"

"I've never seen him working on a bird house. No whittling. No nothing," she admitted, brow furrowing. "He's not even reading. He's just watching cars drive by."

"He dresses like someone who would make bird houses. Washed out blue denim over-alls. A baseball cap. But would you say that he makes the bird houses?"

"Maybe his wife makes them," she theorized.

"Now there's a thought," I replied.

"Somebody else makes the birdhouses," she confirmed, and her mouth tightened. "He just sits out here all day long without a sign to tell how much they are waiting for someone to get curious enough to stop and ask. I wouldn't want to be married to someone like that."

"That's all I was waiting to hear," I said, cranking the ignition. "You have to keep an eye out for someone who looks like he's working but he isn't. Never date a man whose hands are softer than yours either."

"We're not even going to look at the birdhouses?" she asked.

"We've seen enough, haven't we?"

12
Hello, My Brother

He lobs prayers and greetings over his shoulder as he jogs past me in the park, knees lifted high, shoulders balanced in the rhythm of the athletically trained. He calls out to me, "Good morning, Sister."

"Good morning," I call back. And I smile.

This man who is literally a passing acquaintance is full of what I know to be the joy of the Lord, but his is a state of ebullient faith that proper Presbyterians don't express as casually and as uncensored as his standard greeting when I reply, "How are you, sir?"

"Blessed by the Lord," he says with a flash of a grin, and I smile more, and nod vigorously in agreement, but carefully because we have moved into the tricky terrain of testifying. Being a woman raised in a church where women are schooled to keep silent, I'm not good at it.

It's not the church's fault, of course. I have simply not learned how to integrate praising God into my daily discourse. So far on my regular morning walks that intersect with this joyful man's testifying, I have fumbled through a number of stilted replies that good manners train you to say but which don't express what I know too when the spirit in me recognizes the authenticity of the spirit in this man. I am frequently reduced to smiling and nodding, and smiling and nodding. Yes, I smile and nod and try to think of how I can answer him in such a way that honors his good will for it is obvious by his smiling countenance and springy steps that he is fit—both physically and spiritually. He is living out his vocation inside the life of a Christian believer anointed for joy and, as an unstoppable consequence, evangelism.

For inside the life of a Christian believer anointed for joy, he is assured, robust in a love for his neighbors who look like me: a self-conscious plodding walker of a woman who is meditative by temperament and whose vocation in the Lord has placed her Sundays on the pews along with the other frozen chosen: a position we laughingly refer to among ourselves but do not do much to change because being still and reverent are authentic postures in the faith which are genuine, though perhaps not as welcoming and inherently evangelical as this man's openness to strangers.

When we run and walk in the same direction we don't speak, but when we face each other, he calls me "Sister." I am, indeed, moved by his greeting—am drawn not to him and his magnetic personality that has been made so by the changing power of Jesus Christ but by the irresistible love of Jesus himself pouring out of this running man.

I like it when this man calls me Sister. I like that he has no reserve, no caution because of the color of my skin, for we live in a city that has defined boundaries in the past for men and women, black men and white women, and men and women inside the life of churches where roles and authority are delegated and defined by gender and, often, age.

Inside and outside the church, I have mostly known a healthy respect for boundaries—and indeed, heard a sermon last week that warned us that out of respect for our sinful natures we should not be alone with a member of the opposite sex in circumstances that could lead to moral failure.

There is wisdom in that stance but also a kind of suffocating fear that has made me a woman who loves being this running man's sister but so far has failed to call out as loudly as I feel it, "Hello, my Brother."

I want to—but I am still working up to saying "Amen" louder than a whisper after the preacher's prayer.

In the meantime, I am reveling in the good will of this running emissary of the Lord whose robust greeting each day declares to people like me that he has fully accepted the reconciliation of himself to God through a reliance upon the mediator of that reconciliation: Jesus Christ. But because of Jesus Christ, reconciliation can happen each day—every day—to each of us in our running and walking, self-conscious, awkward lives.

13
When God Smiles

If he hadn't been so beaten up, he would have been handsome. However, time and hard work had taken a toll on him, and as a consequence, he was merely ruggedly good looking.

His skin was a weathered tan, his blue eyes well-creased from squinting into sunlight. The hair had once been blond but had grown sandy and grey with time. It had thinned. On the chair beside him was a hat like Crocodile Dundee's. Like Paul Hogan's, his body was lean, for hard work had cost him weight. I could tell from his conversation that he was a roofer.

Beside him, his son sat waiting his turn to take the driver's license test. They talked quietly.

"How old do you think that woman over there is?" He asked his son, nodding toward an attractive lady across the room.

Shrugging his shoulders, the teenager grimaced at the question. "How should I know how old she is?"

"You could guess," his father prompted while keeping his eyes on her.

"I don't know stuff like that."

"Come on. Think."

The blond woman whose age was being assessed was oblivious to their scrutiny. She was having her own conversation with a teenage daughter who was also there to take the driver's test. Oblivious to this pertinent clue that mirrored their situation, the teenage boy clamped his lips and stayed mum—angry at having to take any kind of test.

My curiosity whetted, I scrutinized the blonde in question. Her brown leather sandals framed delicate feet with pink polished toenails. A diamond tennis bracelet accentuated a thin tanned wrist. A French manicure hinted that she did not scrub bathrooms for a living. Belted white shorts and a crisp navy blouse complemented a tidy aerobicized figure. She was attractive in a prosperous, well-groomed way.

The boy's father persisted in his inquiry. "Would you say she's younger than I am?"

"How old are you?" The boy asked.

"You know how old I am," the father said. "I'm forty-five. Would you say she's over forty? Take a good look at her."

The boy shrugged again and looked instead toward the test-giver to see if staring hard would force his turn to come so he could escape this room, the inquisition, and his father.

The weather-beaten man finally answered his own question. "We went to school together. That's how old she is. Graduated high school the same year. But look how she's held her age. When it came to aging, God smiled on her, and He did not smile on me."

Hearing that, I wanted to jump in where angels fear to tread and tell this guy that I thought he was pretty good looking in a beat-up sort of way, but a possible misinterpretation of my unsolicited opinion kept me from it. He might think I was flirting with him, and my intention was not to flirt. He might accuse me of sexual harassment, and pausing a moment to consider whether my attention was tainted with lust, I concluded that my conscience was clean. I found him good looking in the same spirit that he appreciated the tidy blonde. It was unfortunate, I thought, that he could be so complimentary of the woman across the room, and, simultaneously, so harsh when judging himself.

And, aren't we all?

In this burdened body-conscious, politically-correct society, simple discourse has become as dangerous as walking through a mine field. Only the explosives that may go off are not just the predictable behaviors of imperfect people who may well be hard-hearted or discriminatory, but the tortuous self-consciousness of people who are being taught to judge themselves so critically on a daily basis.

I longed to say, 'Man, that lady hasn't been laying shingles on roofs out in the hot sun for the past twenty years. Your body looks like it has, but your worn roughened appearance is no less attractive in its way than her rested, well-groomed one."

But I didn't. Sitting in the room with the blonde, I felt miserably self-conscious and did not want to invite a comparison by this man who was obviously attuned to and appreciative of good-looking women. Next to her, I didn't feel good looking.

She had that well-tended look that I have always wanted and never taken the time or spent the money to achieve.

The room lapsed into silence while the father and mother who had once been school pals waited on their respective son and daughter to take a test that would be a rite of passage on the way to the greater liberty of adulthood.

Those of us who already had the pieces of paper that permitted us the greater freedoms to pursue happiness along with the other liberties of adulthood sat quietly and self-consciously in our chairs.

14
My Cranky Valentine

The gentleman across from me in the hospital waiting room began rummaging in his pants for a pocket knife. His wife started to laugh when he pulled it out and unfolded the miniature screwdriver. "Now, don't you try to fix that coffeepot for those two sweet ladies. You'll just break it worse than it was before."

I looked behind me to see the woman speaking. His wife was a lovely woman with enormous laughing blue eyes and the kind of skin women over 50 don't usually have: firm, smooth, and a healthy pink.

The sick coffeepot in question was beside me on a table. It was in the care of two skittery hospital volunteers, who couldn't get the coffeepot to work. It wasn't an earth-shattering dilemma, but it was mercifully distracting in this hospital waiting room.

Before turning to go into the room where people in medical garb would check her blood pressure and poke her with needles, his wife waved an indulgent hand at me and cautioned teasingly, "Honey, don't you let that old man break the coffeepot any worse than it already is."

I didn't say a word. I know better than to let myself get drawn into an old lovers' quarrel, even a good-natured one. My parents, married for forty years, talk like these two old lovers do. They don't bicker exactly; but they don't bill and coo like the love birds they claimed they once were.

"What do you do?" I asked the would-be coffeepot repairman.

"I'm retired now," he said. "I sold tires." He told me how much he had loved his job, and when he spoke, he slipped into a gentlemanly shyness that harkened back to when he was a boy and awkward in the company of girls. I liked him.

"She," he said, motioning with his head toward the door his wife had exited, "can't stand having me around the house underfoot. Yesterday, I walked out to the back yard where she was to see if I could help her plant an azalea bush. My honeybun looked up at me and said, `What do you think you're doing out here? Do you think I need you for this?'" He laughed with affection when he repeated the conversation.

Do you think I need you for this?

Would my blood run cold if someone I loved said those words to me? His did not. Her words to him sounded harsh to me, but his interpretation of them wasn't. To him, they were words of love. They reminded me of one of my parents' verbal exchanges.

Daddy speaking to Mama: "You don't love me anymore."

Mama: "I love you enough not to kill you even though you're bothering me while I'm working my crossword puzzle."

Daddy: "What do you have to complain about? Who else do you know who has a husband who still writes her love letters?"

Mama: "You copied that last love poem out of a cartoon from the newspaper. Do you think I don't read the newspaper?"

Cackling with glee, Dad rubbed his hands together with satisfaction: "You fell for it just the same, Shorty."

Me: "That's plagiarism, Daddy. You'd get an `F' in English Composition for that."

They both looked at me as if I was crazy. Mine was not an appropriate comment to make to two people wrestling to continue creating who they are as a couple.

Do psychologists have a name for people who can love each other all their lives without needing therapy?

I studied the retired tire salesman across from me. He was still fiddling with his pocket knife and eyeing the sick coffeepot. I could see an eagerness in him to fix it and prove his wife wrong, because then he would have something to tease her about later.

When his eyes met mine, I did his wife a favor and shook my head from side to side. He risked a sheepish grin and slipped the knife back into his pocket.

I saw his eyes flit anxiously to the clock. *Where was his wife? What was taking so long?* "Everyone told me I wouldn't be able to stand being home every day. But the second morning, I adjusted," he said. "No phone ringing off the wall. No flat tires to fix. Just her to put up with." His eyes went to the clock again. *Where was she?*

The two hospital volunteers, who had broken the coffeepot, clucked sympathetically. It was their job to be sympathetic to someone in pain. But this man's statement wasn't an admission of the kind of pain they were thinking about. It wasn't codependency, not misplaced anger, not even the announcement of an armed truce between two people who have decided to stick it out till death they did part. It was a declaration of his undying love. It was the real thing, and time hadn't broken it.

Other than the coffeepot doing fruitless groaning, nothing in this room where people who love each other wait, needed fixing.

15
Fever Pitch

"He was sick all last week, and you know what that's like."

I did not.

"He said he didn't have an appetite, which is just his way of saying that he won't eat anything normal. You know what that means?"

I grunted ambiguously into the telephone. It was a sufficient response to keep my friend talking about her ailing husband.

"Well, three meals a day, every day he was sick I had to think of something special to fix for him to eat. And, of course, he couldn't come to the table to eat it. Wherever he was sitting, I had to take his food to him and stand next to him while he ate the first bite because it might be too hot for him, and he didn't have the breath, he said, to blow on his own food. So, I blew on it for him, and told him, "Don't burn your tongue, now darlin'.

"Do you know how hard that is—to blow on someone else's food without spitting? I won't be winning any assertiveness training awards from Gloria Steinem, but then, that woman is not practiced at being married, so she doesn't really know what it's like here in the trenches.

"It's okay to fight for equal rights when your man is well enough to stand being told he's wrong, but a woman can't argue with a man when he's sick because he's likely to curl up in a ball and die on her, and then she's stuck with the memory that she killed him."

Before I could verify that my friend really thought her husband might kick the bucket if she told him he was wrong, she offered another revelation.

"I can't tell you how many times I've imagined myself standing next to my husband's grave as we lowered his casket into the ground, and I'm thinking, 'This is my fault. If I could just have told him he was right one more time while he was sick, he might still be alive today.' Anyway, when he's ailing, I cook myself crazy trying to please him."

I thought that was an accurate diagnosis because she sounded crazy to me.

"Of course, it's a whole different ball game when a woman gets sick," she declared. "He'll contradict you night and day because he thinks he knows what's good for you. I learned early on that when I'm sick, I might as well resign myself to dying or living on Saltine crackers because if I'm depending on my husband for food, I might as well join the birds outside and start hunting for worms.

"The last time I had a cold all I asked of my Sweet Thang was that he go to the store and buy me a can of chicken noodle soup. I begged him to buy me a simple can of chicken noodle soup, because that's all I thought I could swallow.

"Do you know what he came back with? He brought back a can of that chunky beef stew with lardlike potatoes. He told me that the beef would be better for me than the chicken, and when I told him that I did not think I could swallow hunks of grease, he actually told me I was being a difficult patient.

"To make up with him I had to tell him he was right one more time by eating every drop of that soup that he kept explaining he had made a special trip to the grocery store to buy. And you bet your life I couldn't stay sick for long. When he said he was going to go and buy me a case of that beef stew to last the week, I got myself out of the bed and told him I was all right, which I guess means that in his own way, he did help me get well.

"He called me a few minutes ago. This was his first whole day back to work after being sick, and he said he was coming home for lunch and asked what I was making. I couldn't believe my ears. I don't cook a hot lunch except when he's here, and you'd think after all these years he would know that. I didn't tell him that though, because the news might have put him into a relapse, and I don't think I could live through that. I tried to break it to him easy. I said, 'Don't you and the boys eat barbecue at The Smokehouse on Mondays?'

"He said in that low pitiful voice men get sometimes, 'I want to come home.' You know how a man can say those words?"

"No, I don't," I replied truthfully. "I'm not married, remember?"

"I am," she replied thoughtfully. "And I love Sweet Thang to death, and I'm glad he's well again, but when he gets here, I may have to shoot him."

16
Missing Piece of Nora's Cake

Whenever someone dies in our hometown, Nora, my parents' friend, takes over one of her famous tube-shaped apricot nectar cakes with a fat piece missing. Nora does what every other cake baker would like to do: she samples her cake before she gives it away. That way she can fall asleep that night knowing that there wasn't some dark, damp uncooked spot in the center which proved either that she was an impatient cook or that her oven had cooked too slowly.

I know this about Nora's apricot nectar cakes although she isn't a friend of mine directly. My mother and dad tell me that Nora does this for every reception that follows the funeral of a friend. She baked one to take to my uncle's funeral last year, but I didn't taste it. My folks say it's fruity, tart though sweet. They should know. The number of funerals that Nora and my parents attend is considerable.

Funerals are a mainstay of social life here in our town and the subject for many a conversation in my parents' home. My sixty-two-year-old daddy and my fifty-five-year-old mother are big believers in being prepared for death. They have owned burial plots for years—are two of a very few number of people, I'm sure, who have owned spare burial plots, which they have given away through the years to a couple of needy dead people. Their tombstones have been up long enough to have vines growing over them. The only things missing from the granite slabs are the dates of the deaths. I'm reminded frequently that this pertinent information will have to be added afterwards. I do not like to hear this and try to change the subject. My parents never do. They welcome the opportunity to explore the options inherent in the after-death experience: the funeral.

A couple of months ago, an audacious funeral salesman made the mistake of going by my parents' home on a sales call. My folks invited the funeral salesman to come on inside.

Comfortably situated on the sofa, they interviewed the funeral salesman aggressively, compared what they had already reserved for themselves to the package he was selling, received willingly his brochures, and sent him on his way. Then, because they are thorough investigators, they paid a surprise call on him at his business establishment—the funeral home.

They were shocked at the high price of his poorly constructed caskets and full of self-congratulations that they had foreseen the terrible inflation of funeral costs long ago and bought the only real insurance—a prepaid funeral. They left certain in their souls that the funeral salesman's proposal was, if not crooked, certainly over-priced.

Through the week, they warned all their friends about that guy in the dark blue suit going from door to door in this small town attempting to prey on people who would eventually die. They warned me. No one is going to come to our town and get away with selling an over-priced funeral. There are just too many comparison shoppers here, although my parents, the youngest of the crowd, are the acknowledged experts on funeral preparedness.

"You wanna go and see where our plots are again?" my father inquired once more.

"Nope. Sure don't."

"The time's gonna come and you're not gonna remember where to plant us."

I laughed. "I don't know why you're going to so much trouble. I'm just going to plant you out in the back yard so I won't have to drive into town to put fresh flowers on your graves. I'm thinking I'll put you right out back underneath the magnolia tree. There's plenty of room for both you and mom. I may not even have to buy flowers. Those magnolias will bloom and get ripe and fall right on top of your graves. I tell you what: I'll even turn up the TV at five o'clock so Mother can still listen to Jeopardy."

What could be more natural?

Sometimes when my father initiates this familiar dialogue, I change the plan and say, "I'm gonna stick you out there alongside Still Creek so you can keep those beavers that you like so well company."

My father hates it when I describe my alternative scheme, though he plays along. "Now, don't go be doing that. We'll be washing up every time those beavers rebuild that blasted dam and the rains come in too heavy."

We laugh again, and Mom and Dad file away the details of our conversation so they can tell them to Nora, who will enjoy the story. They fret though that I haven't actually heard any of the real plans they've been making.

I have. Dad insists that when his time comes a recording of Jeanette McDonald and Nelson Eddy singing "Sweet Mystery of Life" be played. He's not joking. He loves that song.

And I do know right where those grave plots are, and I recall that we will have to order the grave opened, but we must not let them do that on a Sunday because grave diggers get time and a half that day.

I do know they've saved an extra grave plot for me; and when they remind me, I take the cue and assure them brightly, "I feel just fine. Couldn't feel better."

They like to hear the report of my good health. None of their friends will ever admit to feeling well, and when I do, they have good news to pass on to their friend Nora.

"Our baby's just fine, Nora. She's doing just fine. She says she's gonna put us out by the creek when our time comes."

This very morning, Nora and Mom and Dad attended two funerals. They went over to the funeral home at ten to pay their respects to a departed church friend and discovered that their insurance agent had also died and was going to be buried an hour later. They just stayed on for that one.

Usually, while they are away at one of their gatherings, I read the obituary of the newly deceased, and today I saw that the father of one of my high school friends had also died. I recognized all of the names of the survivors and wondered if Luanne had to help choose the coffin and buy the concrete vault. *Did Luanne know about the grave diggers?*

Suddenly, I hoped her mama had a friend who would take over a warm cake with a piece missing: a hole she wouldn't try to disguise by pushing the ends together. I wanted all grieving people to have friends like Nora who represent that sweet mystery of living called loving your neighbor as yourself.

It seems more and more fitting to me to think of that missing piece of Nora's cake as an undisguisable void in a circle of friends and relatives who move faithfully from house to house in times of mourning, remembering who their friend was, what he did on his off days, what she liked to cook and wear, and how she couldn't resist putting on fresh eyeliner while the collection was being take up in church. I'll recall how everyone who partook of that apricot nectar cake time after time was participating in a silent communion, as if with every sweet tart bite, they could rob death of some of its sting.

When Nora's gone, I'll remember her cakes and her husband who demanded his share of a warm piece first as his price for having to live with the tempting smell of it baking.

When my parents are gone, we'll have the stories of their love to tell, of their funeral preparations to recount amongst ourselves, recalling with affection how once they bested the final enemy, not death, but that overpriced funeral salesman.

I shall remember glumly reading the announcement that Luanne's daddy had died, ignoring the part that said he was sixty-two, the same age as my own dad.

When my father came home from that double funeral, I told him about Luanne's dad and about how Luanne and I were best friends in eighth grade. Dad remarked, "I hope that man had a concrete vault already bought. You know the price of concrete has gone sky high."

"I doubt Luanne gives a damn about the price of concrete," I said.

My father cannot imagine anyone not caring about the price of concrete.

My mother stole a minute away from watching Jeopardy to tell me not to say "damn" out loud in her house, and then she settled back for Double Jeopardy, a sturdy woman unafraid of death. She is at peace about how her daughters will live with grief. She and Dad have done everything they know to teach us how to accept the unacceptable.

They have already paid the bills.

They have set good examples of being faithful friends to their friends.

They have shown us how to mourn—by remembering the good in each other, making light of the bad, and by laughing at the absurdities of human nature. All we girls have left to do is order the dates inscribed on those tombstones already standing on the grave plots they have owned for years. Then, I imagine we'll listen to Nelson Eddy and Jeanette

McDonald sing "Sweet Mystery of Life" one more time.

What could be more natural?

17
Her Bodyguard

He stood behind his new bride at the dinner party, wearing the poker-faced expression of a caregiver who feigns invisibility until the patient in his care requires assistance. His too-thin wife sat in the only wing back chair. Her legs splayed comfortably in an uninhibited posture that contrasted with the modest Southern-girl bonnet she wore to hide her bald head. His wife has breast cancer, and this man has become the vigilant caregiver--better, bodyguard--a job that seasoned lovers and good daughters usually adopt.

A former caregiver who spent three years locked inside a house with a father who suffered with and then died from Alzheimer's disease, I watched the bridegroom bodyguard, wondering in what ways his experience was different from mine.

My patient—my father-- lost his mind slowly. He forgot how to behave in public. He drooled and leaked. He got mad at hallucinations that stalked him. Sometimes strangers and his own kin feared him. In his dilapidated state, my father was not attractive to others. The isolation was acute for him and for me and my sisters.

During that time, I learned how to be alone in ways I did not know were possible. I learned how to wait, too. And, I learned how to do different jobs that are part of caregiving for an Alzheimer's patient: cut a man's hair, shave him, pare his nails. I even made friends with his delusions, which appeared as the sun set: "Sundowner's Syndrome," they called it.

I wondered about the new words in this man's life since the diagnosis of his wife's illness, and if he said the new words over to himself outside at night, practicing how to say them calmly when he had to—fearlessly when it mattered most.

A steady stream of well-wishers greeted the couple, attempting the awkward task of offering congratulations on the recent wedding while simultaneously offering words of sincere concern. I watched our mutual friends move through the room, making their way to pay their gentle respects to this sick bride, to embrace her, respectful of that side of her weakened now by muscle loss and radiation burns.

Her bodyguard remained poised behind her, silent, eyes disciplined and deliberately opaque so that no one could read his mind and see.... what?

My eyes used to hide the secret life a caregiver lives. It is one of disciplined optimism. Of ready service. Of dread and hope living side by side. Of being terribly alone while always in the company of someone who was going to die no matter what I did as his caregiver.

'This caregiver has a more promising future,' I thought. The prognosis was good. Whenever possible one or the other of them said to anyone listening, "Get that mammogram. It's life or death. We caught it early."

The treatments were working. And they had a network of friends who supported them. Those were the facts.

But was he still afraid? Did he have job pressures as he juggled caregiving with making a living that supported him and his wife? Did he feel all alone though, as a caregiver, he was rarely alone?

The buffet dinner was finally ready, and we all rose. His patient moved serenely through the crowd, a bride welcoming the guests at the reception. He followed her, nodding as others assured her that she looked great. She fixed her own plate, adding spoonsful of this and that, and I saw him watch and take deep breaths as she took more food. 'Good, good. Eat more,' he thought. 'Eat as much as you can.'

He forgot to make his own plate as he followed her. He smiled appropriately at friends who patted her or nodded some silent intention of good will toward him, but the smile never made it to his eyes. Compliments brought the bride closer to him, however. She leaned gratefully toward her husband, patted his chest, and called him her hero. The look in his eyes remained the same.

Suddenly, we were together in a corner, and I told her what everyone else had been saying-- that she looked lovely--and then I turned to him, the male counterpart to a focused, intense caregiver life I have survived and still think about as if it was a mysterious part of my past that doesn't need to be solved—just understood more and more as time passes in this new state the obituary named as being a survivor.

"How are *you*?" I asked him. It sounded like a casual question, the kind of question that everyone asks everyone. It is a question that always surprises caregivers because it is such a radical shift in focus.

This man, whose gaze has been opaque all evening, answered the question I had been wanting to ask about whether the caregiver experience is different for men than it is for women. It is the same.

When addressed as a human being rather than as the silent stoic caregiving hero, this bodyguard answered the question with the same old word women caregivers use in order to save their strength for later. "Fine," he said, but his eyes filled with tears.

18
What He Wants for Father's Day

Her hand rested intimately on the top of his thigh near his outstretched hands. She wanted him to hold hers. He didn't. Her body pulsed toward his possessively, needing something that wasn't passion. She wanted his attention. The more attentive she was, the quieter he became. Her husband Tony was between us in the middle seat of a plane, and he needed some space and quiet.

Having been on a cruise ship for two weeks and in transit for almost 20 hours heading home, I needed some too. I closed my eyes, tuning out the drama of a husband and a wife working out their relationship, which I had been privy to while we had waited together in the Detroit airport.

During that lay-over the good wife told me to move so that her husband could have my seat. I moved, but her husband didn't take the arranged seat. Instead, Tony dropped to a crouch against the wall opposite me, balancing on his heels, his gaze veiled.

Feeling him retreat, she tried harder to woo him back to the present moment with her. She offered some deluxe trail mix. He stared straight ahead, not hearing her until she finally gave up and focused her motherly attentions on her dad, who had been gone too long (I was worried!) in the men's room and whose carryon bag needed to be rezipped properly. She fixed it, offering him a glance: *What would you do without me?*

That question underpinned these ministrations. She cared deeply about both her father and her husband, and she wanted to help them! They didn't want to be helped.

Some men—the strong, silent type especially--would rather bleed or starve than be bandaged or fed in public by a self-appointed doting mother. Only they don't tell her that. Instead, they don't sit where told to or they try to escape some other way.

The week before I had seen an older daddy who walked with a cane execute an escape from his daughter who had been mothering him on the cruise ship and on land too in Palermo, one of our ports of call.

With a slightly nicked finger as his excuse, her daddy hurried off alone, he said, to find a Band-Aid at a local pharmacy.

His startled daughter observed as he skedaddled, "Dad can walk awfully fast for a man who uses a cane."

He was running away from his daughter's relentless mothering, not toward a Band-Aid. He didn't return until it was almost time for the bus to come and take us to the ship.

While waiting later near him, that daddy confided to me: "My daughter never leaves me alone."

Seeing a lot of myself in his daughter, I tried to explain us both: "We women like to fuss over our men. We love you and that's how we try to show it."

Our bus pulled up and the good daddy rose and rejoined his daughter, stoically. Before he left, he said: "I don't like to be fussed over."

It was that fatigued tone of voice that foreshadowed the same exasperation I heard on the plane when I first stood up to welcome the good wife and her husband when Zone 1 was allowed to board.

"Hello, Tony," I said.

He did a double take when I used his name, deducing with a resigned sigh, "You've heard my name too much in the airport." He added tiredly in that same tone as the daddy from Palermo, "Me, too."

Then, on the plane he pretended to go to sleep while his wife rustled papers and asked him questions that he answered with his eyes closed.

Tony didn't fully rouse until she spilled her Diet Coke on him; and when he helped to blot up the mess, she beamed to find him so dependable. She didn't see how truly dependable he is. That lucky woman could afford to relax and trust the character of his love—it is enduring. She doesn't need to earn his love or prove hers.

That very tension may well increase on Father's Day. I suspect a lot of men are dreading the wordy greeting cards that they are expected to be touched by and are already bracing to say 'thank you' for gifts that feel more like a burden than a present.

Very soon the good mother from Seat A will go to some trouble and expense to find a gift for each man—her father and her husband, and she will choose a Father's Day card but it won't say this: "Please take the day off from being anybody's father and I will take the day off from acting like your mother—and tomorrow too. And the day after that."

I am convinced good men who don't like a fuss will like that unexpected Father's Day gift of space and quiet more than any shirt, tie, cologne, Band-Aid or bag of premium trail mix.

19
Before there was Mr. Lovejoy... there was this man

I was having dinner at Bucky's bar at the Grand Hotel in Point Clear, Alabama, when I saw an older distinguished man sipping a martini and staring through the back window at the horizon of the Gulf of Mexico as the sun set.

And I knew him—not his name or the name of the woman he was missing and privately toasting with his small sips of that martini. But I knew him, and the concentration of his memories filled the space around him and drew me to him, like a love song. Like the great old love songs I grew up singing. Those songs fit his story.

When I got home, I wrote this story that happened to me when I saw a man whose name came with the sunset and the martini and the black grand piano he kept eyeing longingly: Franklin Lovejoy.

So, in a way this story is autobiographical. I never met the man but Franklin Lovejoy happened to me. LOVEJOY was inspired by a real-life sighting of a man who had been deeply in love and as it turns out with more than one woman.

It's part of the mystery of writing that stories come this way from chance encounters or in this case, a chance sighting. This is Lovejoy's story—and mine, in a way. I hope it will be one you enjoy too.

The love story begins in a Southern church where desire for God is often confused with desire for a lover.

Lovejoy happened to a Southern belle who, at first, admires the eligible older man from afar. Here's a little bit of that first spark between Lovejoy and the woman who, like others, couldn't say no to this man who had a way with the ladies.

20
Bonus Excerpt: Lovejoy

I was past my prime but not yet old when I met my match, Mr. Lovejoy. The distinguished widower had been part of the background of my community, an old Southern church where tradition is as romantic as the scent of magnolia and the fragrance of the gospel is as abundant as the scent of that flower that ladies in social clubs use for tabletop centerpieces.

Through a natural reluctance to join myself to a ladies' social club that defined me by my gender or marital status, I kept myself apart in the Southern society where God had placed me. I lived on the perimeter where spectators observe and often have opinions. In Sunday school I sat near the wall. In church I sat near the back, where I was occasionally shaken out of my church-time reverie when I heard a man belt out "Amen" whenever the preacher made a point that might have gone without attention otherwise.

Heads turned at the sound of one of us agreeing out loud with the preacher. Eyes widened to discern the rebel among us-- the man of the Amen. He wasn't hard to spot. The man who vigorously agreed with the preacher was Franklin Lovejoy, a widower of two years.

A handsome man, Mr. Lovejoy sat by himself five pews up from me, and often I watched with amusement the number of ladies who attempted to establish a stronghold beside this older available man. They came and went. I don't know what he said or didn't say that did not encourage the ladies to return. Some did come back, for a while. There were even some Sunday mornings when a single woman nestled in on Lovejoy's left side and another lady snuggled in on his right.

Sunday mornings became like a soap opera to me. I watched, taking note of the women who came and went while the preacher positioned himself behind the pulpit, oblivious to the sexual tensions brewing in the pews.

Most early morning church goers arrive a quarter to the hour in order to get our preferred pews. For that early rising, we not only win our respective cherished pews but are treated to ten minutes of slow-down-and-get-silent-before God music. After the bell chimes announcing the hour, the preacher stands—often shyly. I never like the preacher more than when he first approaches the pulpit with both diffidence and courage, self-protection and openness. A deep silence comes over him just as he is supposed to say a few words about this and that. Then, in the midst of words about love and mercy and beauty and truth that point us toward the God of Wonders, wonder of wonders, Franklin Delmar Lovejoy, a great encourager of deacons, elders, and younger men who try to preach, would release at exactly the moment when the preacher needed a pat on the back, his signature one-word cheer of encouragement, "Amen."

Instantly that single word created a bridge that connected the preacher to all of us. We were one--created to be one in a breath all together. I marveled at the happening, and kept my eye on Mr. Lovejoy, who made it happen.

He was the only one to do it. (There isn't much talking back to the preacher in our church.) I liked the sound of Lovejoy's voice, too. Often when people are described in terms of their attractiveness or appeal the effect of their voice on you is not mentioned, and it should be. The timber of a voice can be very comforting (or surprising); but in Lovejoy's case, his voice was seductive—head-turning. Irresistible. Preachers who wanted to be great preachers coveted Lovejoy's resonant truth-carrying voice and its stirring effect of commanding attention.

Sometimes I whispered the word "Amen" after Mr. Lovejoy just to hear myself speak in church because mostly women don't speak in church, not in the South, anyway; and if you do, it is to cheer or encourage a man in his walk of faith. And so, I was not skilled in speaking and even kept my ideas to myself, believing, rightly I think—amen? —that I simply don't know enough about anything to have a worthwhile opinion.

However, upon whispering "Amen" after Mr. Lovejoy during the church service, I began to learn the sound of my own voice and the power of agreeing and, sometimes, the extraordinary freedom of disagreeing.

No one was more surprised than I after being on a committee called Tender Mercies that I would one day find myself speaking up loudly and with many more words than the man who said, "Amen." But it was Franklin Delmar Lovejoy who had somehow initiated my freedom of speech.

One amen can cause a ripple effect in others. An amen has the power of contagion.

Mr. Lovejoy had tapped into some kind of unnamed restlessness in me, and his amen had triggered my speaking up in the Tender Mercies meetings. Only my words were not about agreement; they were a loud and serious questioning of perpetuating helplessness in others by helping others too much in the name of Tender Mercies. It is a surprising situation to speak out against giving too much help in the name of mercy in a church where mercy is the sister word for grace. Yet, I without a plan to be one, became that voice of dissent.

My position in the church community changed as a result. It didn't happen the first time I suggested a background check on a stranger who had come in off the street asking for help with his electric bill. I wanted to know if chronically seeking help from neighborhood churches was how he made his living. Later, when one missionary candidate requested plane fare to reach his mission field, I muttered the unpardonable: "That's the place Pat Sajak on "Wheel of Fortune" often sends people as a prize trip when they spell an easy word correctly on the TV game show. I wonder why so many missionaries end up in destinations that are places given away as jackpot prizes on America's game shows."

That's the statement that finally landed me in the dog house outside the perimeter of what is considered good behavior at church. I felt the earth shift under me and heads duck as they calculated how many more months I was scheduled to serve on the Tender Mercies committee before they could finally show me the door. I eyed the door myself, thought about making up a physical condition that I could offer to excuse myself from future committee work; but, in a fit of menopausal madness I spoke to God while looking at myself in the mirror, "What's sinful about having an unpopular opinion?" So, I stayed—mainly to find out what, if anything, would be done about the problem—me.

I walked the widening fault line created by my questions, growing increasingly apart and alone as others who knew of my meddlesome troublemaking began to turn gently to the side when I passed by. You don't have to be formally rebuked at church, put in time out by the elders, or receive a formal letter of warning that you are in danger of excommunication to know you are on the outs with church leadership.

The more powerful event at church is to be very quietly and effectively shunned. Most people leave a church of their own accord as an effect of shunning, sheepishly disappearing into the future with nary a backward glance. But I lived in the neighborhood, and I didn't want to find another church far enough away so that my reputation would not precede me or close enough that people who knew me here would know me there and know about me.

So, I stayed in my pew, whispering "Amen" after Mr. Lovejoy, and keeping my eye on the calendar to count down the days of my impending expiration on the Tender Mercies committee. People do forget, over time. After a while they would forget my trespasses, and in the forgetting, forgive?

That hopeful plan did not stop me from continuing to speak and question spending decisions in committee meetings, however. No matter how many times I gave myself a talking to about being quiet and more agreeable, in the very next meeting someone would paint a scenario that required mercy, an expensive hand out to someone in a sports ministry or to a cowboy on the rodeo circuit who wanted to tell people about the Lawd in between bronco bustin'. That night, I said, "Tell that good ole cowboy if he's not a good enough bronco buster to win the rodeo prize money and support himself with his chosen vocation, maybe he should open a lawn service. Like the Apostle Paul, you can make tents or earn a living cutting yards while you tell homeowners about the Lawd."

I've been witnessed to by a number of lawn mower men, coffee-serving waitresses, and hair-cutting artistes. You can do all kinds of work, testify to the good news that salvation is through faith alone in Jesus, and not take money from the church to say those words wherever you go.

It was a long meeting with lots of sighin'. I ended up sitting by myself at the end of the long conference table, and I understood why. The implications of saying no to people needing tender mercies were not hard to understand. If we stopped giving out the money then the Tender Mercies committee and the person in charge of the committee was out of a job. Then there would be no stories to tell to elicit more contributions from the congregation to give to people who needed money, and down the road after a while, eventually, surely, the gospel.

That was a sticking point, you see. I kept saying, "Tell 'em about Jesus, and then tell them to get a job. After that, teach that working man to tithe and let the Lord show him how to become a good steward of himself, including the gift of labor. Work is a gift. In so many ways, a hand-out is not the gift we think it is."

In the year of the 500th anniversary of the Reformation out of the blue and on a low humidity morning when my freshly trimmed hair with newly added streaks of blonde and a saucy little flip of a curl on the left side of my bangs that "Gives your face a lift, Miss Cindy, so please don't try to iron it out," said my hair dresser, Mr. Lovejoy of the Amen asked me to lunch.

But first, he extricated himself from the presence of a woman I greatly admire who was well groomed, wore taupe tummy control panty hose without gasping for air, could walk in black patent leather high heels without teetering, had thick brown lustrous Grand Ole Opry hair that was immune to humidity, could make small talk better than Paula Deen, and her laugh was a light tinkling sound that made you think of Christmas bells. Mr. Lovejoy excused himself from the lady with the tinkling Christmas bells laugh and asked me—the church leper-- to Sunday lunch.

Thinking that it was about time someone delivered the criticism from above formally that my opinions were proving problematic, I lit up girlishly, automatically, and said, sweetly, with a honeyed smile on my face, "Oh, thank you so much" to his invitation to Sunday lunch in order to get this problem of being rebuked by the leadership behind me. Go ahead, Mr. Lovejoy. Tell me how wrong I am and that I have been excused from further service on the committee, and I will turn the other cheek and disappear like the vapor I am. And in that moment of planning my reply to what he would surely say during lunch, I wondered if much of what I had been saying on the committee was perversely spoken to get myself kicked off the committee so that I didn't have to formally quit.

I hate quitters and deep down I didn't want to be one.

****

Mr. Lovejoy waited for me by the church's side door that led to the street where his car was parked. Holding the heavy wooden door open for me to pass through, he said, his voice more a whisper than a command, "My car is right over there. Country Club okay with you?"

I thought the offer of lunch at the Country Club was unnecessarily generous for a man with the delegated, and I was sure, highly discreet mission to excuse me ever so politely from future church service on the Tender Mercies committee. Elder Lovejoy could have gotten by cheaper and accomplished his task with a standard meat-and-three vegetable lunch at any of the local restaurants where 8.99 was the price of Sunday lunch if you didn't order iced tea.

I routinely drink water with Sunday lunch to save the two dollars for a glass of tea because these small spending decisions that result in savings are how I accumulate enough money to contribute to the Tender Mercies fund. When I don't drink iced tea on Sunday that saved two dollars goes toward missions support, and it matters. I like iced tea. It is my favorite drink; and when I don't drink iced tea, it is my drink offering unto the Lord, a sacrifice in the name of tender mercy. (The church likes to call that kind of giving by other names, but I like to use my own labels!)

A half foot taller than I, Mr. Lovejoy walked silently beside me, careful to have his arm ready for me to hold onto if I needed help balancing on the concrete steps that led to the street where he was parked. In that short walk from the church to his car I was suddenly aware of the fragrance of magnolia. Suddenly I was flooded with the aroma, as if a breeze had wafted through the neighborhood and carried the scent from every tree nearby right to us. When we reached his car, a twelve-year old Buick of hard body and a trusty navy blue, Mr. Lovejoy opened the door for me and waited for me to sit down and swing my legs in and situate them. I have never been very good at being tended to by a man this way, having spent most of my life climbing in and out of cars alone and getting onto and out of chairs without any kind of masculine assistance.

The last time a man helped me with my chair was at the Tender Mercies committee meeting four months ago. Surprised by Dick's sudden help with sitting down, I twisted my foot under the chair, and it had gotten wedged sideways with my ankle straining and my foot bent and turned toward the floor. It took me through the opening prayer and the reading of the minutes from the previous meeting before I could get my foot unstuck. And then my ankle throbbed, and it didn't stop hurting. Upon rising an hour later, I pretended my discomfort was from a leg that had gone asleep, but that wasn't true. I got my foot stuck under the chair when Dick, the man helping me onto and later out of the chair, surprised me both times with his gallantry.

Settling into Mr. Lovejoy's car, I felt a remembered fear of getting hurt and a kind of test being taken about what it means to be a woman with a man, and I didn't know whether or not I was going to fail: I was sure I would.

Lovejoy was not impatient. He let me settle inside the car on the passenger side and arrange my three-year old black leather purse at my feet. Relaxed and patient, he leaned forward smiling, his breath a surprising fragrance of mint and vanilla—what kind of mouth wash is minty vanilla? --smiled at me, warmly, and his eyes, the color of the old South, blue-grey twinkled with amusement. For the strangest second in my life (at that time) I thought Mr. Lovejoy fought the urge to lean in and kiss me. It felt like that, really.

The door closed upon this suspicion of desire, and Mr. Lovejoy walked around the back of the car to reach the driver's side. I was suddenly aware in ways that I had never really waked up to before that I was a woman; and when Mr. Lovejoy positioned himself behind the steering wheel, I saw him not as an attractive elder in my hometown church who was well fixed, well respected, and desired by most of the older single women and lonely widows in the congregation, but as someone much more dangerous.

Franklin Lovejoy was a man with a membership at the Country Club who attended to a woman as if she were a lady, and he was about to buy me lunch. I was sure the ax would ultimately fall and I would soon find myself separated from the Tender Mercies committee; but until it did, I felt weak and kind of excited too. It was a strange feeling, and once I got over being afraid of what

What Makes a Man a Hero?

Mr. Lovejoy would do next, I liked feeling that way.

He drove us the short distance to the Country Club, steering, leading, guiding in ways that made me feel protected and something I hadn't known in a long time and which I did not expect to feel when I early on believed he was going to shepherd me into a more graceful and ladylike silence at church. I felt the most intoxicating sensation of being safe. If danger came, I believed Mr. Lovejoy would stand between me and whatever the danger was. When a man can make you feel safe, he becomes, paradoxically and ironically too, very dangerous. Even the strongest woman becomes weak with a man like that.

Walking up the steps to the Country Club, I began to experience the forgotten feeling of being intoxicatingly and dangerously safe, and when Mr. Lovejoy opened the door for me, I stepped out of the noontime sunlight and into the shadows of the Club's well-appointed lobby. Almost instantly, I was not only safe in his company, I felt at home with him too.

We went from being polite acquaintances to something more just by crossing a common threshold. A friendly rapport settled upon us. We became instantly easy with one another. And I became more curious about him.

Having watched the soap opera called Lovejoy's way with the ladies on Sunday morning from five pews behind, I knew what the back of his head looked like. In the car, I had checked out his profile. He had a nicely shaped head. In the Country Club dining room sitting cross from him at the table I beamed at him in my most friendly way while taking an inventory of his features. His eyes crinkled with good humor; his smile was paradoxically quick and lazy. His hands were gentle and controlled. He was comfortable in his skin. At ease, he draped his thick white cloth napkin across his knees, and I immediately did the same thing. He wasn't wearing a wedding band.

Three people attended us: the man who escorted us to the table, the lady who brought the basket of warm breads, and Alfred the waiter who announced that he "Would be taking care of us."

Just as I was going to wave away the offer of iced tea and request my usual frugal glass of water, Lovejoy raised one of his musical hands—yes, like a conductor's, he could lead music with those hands-- and he ordered a mimosa for us each, an unexpected treat. Looking up at Alfred, Lovejoy said without asking me if I agreed, "The lady and I will not be an in hurry today. We are getting to know one another."

Lovejoy's voice was warm and laced with amusement and entreaty to the server: Be on our side, won't you?

"Understood, sir," Alfred replied, bowing slightly, and he smiled first at him and then winked at me, an impertinence I wouldn't have understood if Mr. Lovejoy hadn't leaned toward me slightly just as the golfers outside on the Country Club golf course moved out toward the first hole and said, "Alfred understands what you do not yet realize." Lovejoy took a measured sip of the ice water already on the table before setting the glass back down. Holding my gaze, he said easily, "I want you."

I waited and then finally asked, "Want me to do what?"

He stifled an amused chuckle and blotted his lips with the white cotton napkin, taking his time amending his statement. "I mean that I want to court you."

The second statement was no less surprising than the first. And what did he expect me to say or do? I took a nervous sip of ice water and choked. Coughing bought me some time to think, but it didn't do any good. I couldn't think of anything to say, which was apparently okay with him.

His gaze held mine. I didn't blink either, having grown up in the South where we typically for fun try to stare someone else down. We can also for just a little while read someone else's mind that way. Holding his gaze, I saw that Mr. Lovejoy wasn't asking my permission. He was stating his plan.

His blue grey eyes were rich and warm and amused by my surprise.

Immediately, I dropped my gaze and saw the sleeve of his blue striped seersucker suit moving dangerously close to the small saucer of butter rosettes, 'Little boutonnieres of butter,' I thought, and I would have tried to say something to warn him about the butter just about to get on his sleeve, but the mimosas arrived, icy orange juice frothy with chilled champagne. I don't like a mimosa more than iced tea, but I do like mimosas.

Lovejoy signaled gratitude to Alfred who had brought them. Then he lifted his glass toward me, and I, a long-time imitator of others and trained in the South to be responsive and polite, lifted my glass too.

Lovejoy touched the base of his flute to mine. When I allowed that, it felt to him—and to me, too—as if I had in my silent way as I did at church, mumbled "Amen" to his announcement that he wanted to court me, and my first sip of the frothy aperitif was a polite assent to his plan.

His words bubbled inside of me.

The words "court you" were as old-fashioned as he was, and while I sipped my mimosa, I wondered exactly what he had meant. I concluded that I didn't know. Date? Keep company with? Sit next to in church? What exactly did "court you" mean?

Elder Franklin Lovejoy was in no hurry to elaborate. We ate slowly as if he hadn't said anything at all. The food was remarkably good. We were served small green salads with hearts of palm, candied pecans, sunflower seeds, all spritzed (doused is too strong a verb for how little dressing was used) in a raspberry vinaigrette. Next, Alfred brought us sautéed shrimp and steaming buttery grits. I have always hated shrimp and grits, (Those two things are too pale to go together!), but these were rather tasty.

Then, Lovejoy insisted I try the bread pudding with whiskey sauce. "It's more of a souffle than a dense heavy bready pudding that you might be expecting," he promised. "New

Orleans could be inspired by this chef's recipe for bread pudding."

I didn't say no to the bread pudding.

Alfred brought it from the dessert table, and placed two steaming bowls in front of us. I could smell the whiskey. Lovejoy inhaled and grinned. He waited for me to spoon the first bite. I did. The warm whiskey sauce dribbled down my chin. Lovejoy leaned over and daubed my face with his own thick cloth napkin. The quick intimacy of his action embarrassed me.

"Puddin' looks good on you," he assured me. His voice was laced with hidden meanings, and his eyes teased me to laugh at myself.

I was able to smile, but just barely. I applied myself to finishing the dessert, not looking up until I had eaten it all. When I finally did sit back to face him, Lovejoy smiled broadly, "I like a woman who really eats on a date instead of just toying with her food."

We were on a date! Until he said those words, I did not know that.

"I love to eat," I replied with enthusiasm.

"One of the great pleasures in life," he replied. "But there are others that I would like to share with you." His eyes dared me to be curious.

I smiled tremulously, cautiously, taking deep breaths and wondering if I should grab my purse and make a run for the front door. Sensing my desire to escape the dangerous safety he offered, Lovejoy suggested a drive in the country. Before I could say, 'I usually take a nap on Sunday afternoon,' he finessed the bill, and quietly escorted me back to his car, which he had parked in the shade.

We exited the Country Club's parking lot onto a city road that soon becomes a country lane, heading left instead of right. Five miles later we were still going south.

"I've a good mind to take you to the beach and give you supper at dusk at the Grand Hotel, but I suspect we would both be kicked out of the church for that detour." He looked at me archly, his oceanic eyes twinkling mischief.

"Have you been to The Grand and seen the sun set over the water? It falls fast, a red ball in the sky, sitting at the horizon until it disappears. But before then, you can be a part of the water, the sky, know the motion of the fish and the flight of birds that are fishing the waters and see in the distance the City of Mobile and beyond. You can see the whole world from there if you know how to look for it," Lovejoy promised me, and then I looked into his eyes and saw it all right then in his eyes just as he described it.

My mouth went dry, and I scooted over and hugged the passenger door. I had never met a man who had the whole world in his eyes and knew just what he wanted. No one had ever wanted me like this before and certainly not a man who could have his pick of the ladies at church.

He kept talking. "I would like to take you there on our honeymoon after I have courted you a while and after you have learned to trust me. That will happen," Lovejoy prophesied with conviction. His hands were easy on the steering wheel, and I wondered if he had ever trained horses or sailed boats that required bridles, cords, and ropes being pulled and adjusted.

He did not look at me when he said those words, but I studied him. His face was friendly with shadows and light. Once upon a time I had studied art in college; and in that instant, I wanted to draw him. Yes, I wanted to capture Lovejoy's likeness in my hands. I hadn't drawn anyone in years, and I felt my hand itch to hold a pencil and catch his likeness. I drummed the top of my thigh instead, and he asked me without looking over, "Are you nervous about something?"

I could only shake my head in reply, and though he did not look at me directly I felt that he understood something true about the drumming of my fingers and what they actually meant. It would take me almost five years to understand that wanting to draw Lovejoy was actually the beginning of my desire for him. But then, in that first excursion, I only thought of drawing as a reflex, an impulse, some echo from my youth when I was a girl who had liked to draw and believed in her innocence that a future should accommodate the report of beauty's presence created in art.

Strangely, my thrumming fingers started a rhythm that triggered music in him.

He began to hum an old song that I hadn't heard in years. I think it was an old Perry Como song. Later, I would pay attention to the songs that Lovejoy hummed absentmindedly, as a way, I thought, to figuring out what he was secretly thinking, but I didn't know that then. I just thought he sounded happy. I recalled that I liked Perry Como's voice and music, and I tried to let my legs relax because I couldn't cross them in the car. I wanted my legs to behave themselves and rest in a ladylike position, ankles crossed, black polyester skirt tucked modestly over my knees. Through will alone, I made my hands be still in my lap, but it was hard.

I was wrestling with self-consciousness when Mr. Lovejoy steered the car over on the side of the road and pointed to an old farm house that was sitting high up on a small hill surrounded by pecan trees and one lone magnificent magnolia tree. "I have seen pictures of that house over time. Some photographer has made it his life's work to record the deterioration of that home place by taking pictures of it. Look at it now. I come here to visit it from time to time. It feels like an old friend. Do you know what I mean?"

I didn't have a clue, but I looked dutifully out the window and nodded the way Southern women often nod agreeably in response to questions about famous paintings in museums that are supposed to be admirable because they are famous (but really Van Gogh's dark painting of "The Sower" is just plain ugly!), about annual football games between longtime competitors and about which I don't care (if that's the thrill of victory or the heartbreak of defeat, I don't get that either), and in the produce department when someone asks me, "Is this cantaloupe ripe?" nodding happens then, too.

"That house reminds me of Faulkner's "A Rose for Emily". Do you remember the story?" Lovejoy moved his right arm out and slipped it loosely across the back of the front seat. His fingers toyed with the under curls at the back of my neck. I have a good bit of natural curl (been ironing and trying to straighten out my hair for years), and when I perspire those tendrils on the back of my neck don't just stand up, they spiral out of control. I was sweating and curling riotously about my forehead and at the back of my neck and hoping Lovejoy wouldn't feel the beads of perspiration there. So unladylike!

I concentrated on the magnificence of that magnolia tree. It was like I had never seen a magnolia tree before, but I had. This tree was different, alive, fulsome, pulsing with a kind of romantic aura that until that moment I had not experienced. The branches were full of the most marvelous white flowers. I marveled that whoever owned this tree must not have any socializing friends who needed flowers for tabletop centerpieces or it would have been more pruned of its sumptuous white blossoms and large waxy green leaves. Though the car window was tightly closed, I thought I could smell the blossoms from inside where the interior of the car was growing warmer. Mr. Lovejoy had turned off the engine and with it the air conditioner. I was hot.

"Make no mistake about what is going on here," Lovejoy said softly, his voice a whispered confession in my left ear.

"The tree has so many flowers," I remarked, and my throat was now sandpaper dry. I couldn't remember the Faulkner story exactly, but I resolved to read it again soon so I could catch up with Mr. Lovejoy's observation.

His hand clasped the back of my neck lightly and one finger stroked the nape. My head ducked when he touched me. His other hand moved around my face. Using two cool fingers he tapped my chin and turned my face toward his.

"It isn't a complicated idea once you hear it. You didn't exactly hear me before, though I think you truly liked the bread pudding. I simply want you." And then he leaned forward and kissed me almost on the lips.

Startled, I moved my head slightly, and his kiss landed near the corner of my mouth instead. This has happened to me many times in my life, but I suspect, not often to Mr. Lovejoy. He did not lose his focus.

"What are you afraid of?" he asked, while he cocked his head and contemplated making another try at the kiss.

I couldn't keep my head still any more than I could my right hand, which had begun to squeeze my thigh hard. I was trying to hold onto something: myself.

I stole a glance at him, considered the question to be a dare, and decided to call him on it. He eyed me quizzically, waiting for me to signal something else, so I smiled.

He kissed me again, and this time, I did not jerk away.

He smiled more to himself than at me after the second kiss, and if he had been a younger man, I would have considered that smile a show of conceit, but in the 12-year-old Buick beside an overladen magnolia tree next to a decrepit house that reminded him of Faulkner's story, I thought he just looked pleased with us both. I fought the urge to press my fingertips against my lips to see if the imprint of his mouth was still there, and after a while I could fight it no longer. That man could kiss, and as he drove us home, the memory of it ached. I turned my head to stare out the window so that he could not see my face and the mark of his lips on my mouth, which was burning.

Humming a Frank Sinatra song now, Lovejoy drove me back to my car where I had left it at the church and asked me if I would be present that night for evening Vespers. In a fit of self-preservation, I shook my head no, no, I would not be anywhere in his proximity, for by then the scent of him and the odd mix of safety and danger had caused me to fear for my life.

He smiled genially, a study in patience and optimism. I liked his mouth, the shape of his lips, the taste of mint and vanilla. My face was stony with these realizations of desire.

Back in my own car and as I drove away toward my home, I saw Mr. Lovejoy in the rear-view mirror, and he didn't wave or anything. He just remained there watching, standing guard by the church, and I thought of Fitzgerald's Gatsby, not Faulkner's Emily at all. I pressed the gas pedal hard, zooming away from his declaration of desire.

21
Books by Daphne Simpkins

Short Adventures of Mildred Budge

    Miss Budge Goes to Fountain City

    Miss Budge In Love

    The Mission of Mildred Budge

Long Adventures of Mildred Budge

    Mildred Budge in Cloverdale

    Mildred Budge in Embankment

Essay Collections

    Blessed: stories about caregiving

    What Al Left Behind: Life after Alzheimer's

Other novels

    Christmas in Fountain City

    Lovejoy: a novel about desire

Memoirs

    A Cookbook for Katie

    The Long Good Night

Biography

    Nat King Cole: An Unforgettable Life of Music (for children)

About Daphne Simpkins

Daphne Simpkins has been writing about life in the South for most of her adult life, and now that journey has extended to write about the life of a fictional retired Alabama school teacher, Mildred Budge who is also a full-time church lady. This series of books includes two collections of short stories, a stand-alone Christmas story, and two novels—the third novel due out soon.

Before Daphne became a novelist full-time, she wrote essays and many of these were published in many fine newspapers in America and the United States. These included **The Chicago Tribune, The Atlanta-Journal Constitution, The Baltimore Sun, The St. Petersburg Times, The Miami Herald**, and in Canada, **The Christian Courier.** She has also been published in **The Christian Century**.

A former writing teacher at Auburn University Montgomery, Daphne
is an active member of the Alabama Humanities Foundation's speakers bureau.

Daphne Simpkins

Connect with Daphne Simpkins on Twitter, Linkedin.com or Facebook

Printed in Great Britain
by Amazon